VROOM
with a view

PETER MOORE

BANTAM BOOKS

LONDON • TORONTO • SYDNEY • AUCKLAND • JOHANNESBURG

VROOM WITH A VIEW
A BANTAM BOOK: 9780553816372

Originally published in Great Britain by Bantam Press,
a division of Transworld Publishers

PRINTING HISTORY
Bantam Press edition published 2004
Bantam edition published 2005

3 5 7 9 10 8 6 4

Set in 11.5/16pt Goudy by
Falcon Oast Graphic Art Ltd.

Bantam Books are published by Transworld Publishers,
61–63 Uxbridge Road, London W5 5SA,
a division of The Random House Group Ltd.
Addresses for companies within The Random House Group Limited
can be found at: www.randomhouse.co.uk/offices.htm

Printed and bound in Great Britain by
Cox & Wyman Ltd, Reading, Berkshire.

The Random House Group Limited supports The Forest Stewardship
Council (FSC), the leading international forest certification
organisation. All our titles that are printed on Greenpeace approved
FSC certified paper carry the FSC logo. Our paper procurement
policy can be found at www.rbooks.co.uk/environment

Peter Moore is an itinerant hobo who is lucky enough to be able to support his insatiable travel habit through writing. Author of the bestselling *No Shitting in the Toilet*, which grew from his award-winning website of the same name, as well as *The Wrong Way Home*, *The Full Montezuma* and *Swahili for the Broken-hearted*, Peter is the voice of independent travel in both Australia and the UK. A former advertising copywriter and website designer, he has visited ninety-two countries on his travels. When he is not lugging his senselessly overweight back-pack through Third-World nations, Peter can be found at home in Sydney watching *Neighbours*. Sad, really.

Praise for Peter Moore's travel writing:

'Peter Moore is the genuine article, a traveller's traveller . . . Thoroughly enjoyable . . . Inspirational stuff' *FHM*

'Moore's a sharp observer of the bizarre . . . Read, enjoy, escape' *Maxim*

'Moore writes in a racy, witty style that has no pretensions or self-censorship . . . this book is a hilarious read and fits snugly into any pack' *TNT* Magazine

'Just don't read it in public if you'd prefer not to be caught laughing out loud' *Lonely Planet* newsletter

'A perceptive, subversive and hilarious book'
Sydney Morning Herald

'It will certainly make you laugh' *Sunday Mirror* (Book of the Week)

'An amusing account of forging a relationship in the most challenging of circumstances. Coupled with Moore's seemingly incongruous mix of incisive comments and obscure observations, it all makes for a highly entertaining read' *Later*

'For its irrepressible humour and range of experiences . . . Peter Moore's *The Full Montezuma* is a welcome new addition to the (travel) genre' *Canberra Times*

'Moore is an amiable Aussie with a laidback approach and a chatty humorous writing style – probably just as well given the trip he had' *The Big Issue in the North*

Also by Peter Moor

THE WRONG WAY HOME
THE FULL MONTEZUMA
NO SHITTING IN THE TOILET
SWAHILI FOR THE BROKEN-HEARTED

and published by Bantam Books

To the desire of my heart

Contents

ACKNOWLEDGMENTS

Love and support from the usual suspects: Lorraine and Phil Petersen, Les and Judy Moore, and my sisters, Lesley-Ann Rosenberg, Vanessa Howard and Melinda Moore. And the kids – Jessica Howard, Amanda Howard and James Howard, Taylor Black and Harrison Black, and Kai Moore.

A big word of thanks as well to Gianni Giovenzana, or Ian de Beer, as he likes to call himself on eBay. Gianni sold me my Vespa, and if it wasn't for his extraordinarily generous 'after-sales service' my trip may have never even got started. Thanks, Gianni, and good luck with your new life.

I owe Filippo Lulli and Marco Quaretta a huge thank you. They got my bike going again when all looked lost. And, thanks to these guys showing me around Livorno, I am now convinced it is one of the greatest cities in Italy. Anyone who has ever been to Livorno will realise what an extraordinary achievement that is. One thing no one needs convincing of is that Marco is the world's best Vespa restorer.

Back at Random House Australia it's thank yous all round to Allison Brennan, my longest-serving publicist, as well as Jude McGee and Fiona Henderson, for wrestling this book into shape. Hi to Trish Tribe on reception, who should get a commission for recommending my books to people who ring up.

At Transworld UK a hearty cheers to Larry Finlay, Patrick Janson-Smith, Simon Taylor, Richard MacDonald, Garry Perry, Marina Vokos, Brad Rose and Terry Pink. That I consider all these people friends tells you what sort of publisher they are.

Of course, it goes without saying how much I owe my agents, Fiona Inglis in Australia and Antony Harwood in the UK. Their negotiating skills mean I no longer have to write brochures for golf resorts.

Finally, and most importantly, a big thank you to my beautiful wife, Sally Wray. We were married shortly after she spent a couple of weeks with me in Tuscany, so a word of warning, guys: that's the effect Italy can have on a relationship. The first few months couldn't have been too much fun for her – I transform into a grumpy old bastard when I write – but she accepted it with good grace and humour. Thanks, sweetie.

PROLOGUE

It was a late-night television commercial that finally drove me to pursue a long-held dream of riding around Italy on a Vespa. Not one spruiking a CD of Dean Martin's Italian Love Songs for $19.95 plus postage and handling. Rather, it was a ninety-second spot for Tae Bo fitness tapes.

Tae Bo is a fitness regime developed by a bloke called Billy Blanks. It combines elements of Tae Kwon Do and kickboxing and is very popular with the kind of Hollywood celebrities who appeared briefly on *Baywatch*, usually as a person drowning. On this particular night Mr Blanks was spruiking his entire range of Tae Bo videotapes. There was Tae Bo Standard, featuring the above-mentioned celebrities in Lycra, and Tae Bo for

Kids, featuring precocious children cutely punching and kicking. Then there was Tae Bo Gold, featuring old people in nursing homes feebly throwing punches from their beds while nurses supported their backs, scattering the tubs of custard they'd been given for lunch. When the voice-over guy announced that Tae Bo Gold was for 'the over-forties' I sat up, scattering the crisps I'd been eating, pretty much in the manner of the old dears on the ad. I was only months away from entering Tae Bo Gold territory myself.

I hadn't been particularly worried about turning forty. In fact, I'd read a newspaper article only the week before that declared it the new thirty. I'd lived my life pretty much as I'd wanted to, working for myself and travelling the world. And with a few travel books under my belt, I had at least some achievements I could be proud of. But there were still things that I wanted to do, goals I'd set myself yet to be scored, and riding around Italy on a Vespa was one of them. The Tae Bo ad made me realise that if I wasn't careful my Italian Vespa fantasy would remain just that – a fantasy. A deeply cherished and richly embroidered one, to be sure, but a fantasy nonetheless.

The idea to ride around Italy on a Vespa had first come to me as a teenager. It was a wet Sunday afternoon and I was watching TV. Weekend television in the seventies in Australia usually meant a Jerry Lewis movie or, if you were really unlucky, the twenty-fifth re-run of an Abbott and Costello flick. But that day some inspired soul at TCN 9 decided to show an old black and white Italian movie starring Sophia Loren.

To this day I can't recall which movie it was. I have zero recall of the plot and couldn't tell you for the life of me which other actors were in it. But I do remember with startling clarity that it involved Sophia riding a Vespa around the cobbled streets of a tiny Italian village, and that the grainy image stirred something in me. There, on the screen of our battered Grundig, I saw the epitome of style, sophistication and drop-dead gorgeousness. I also realised with a Neanderthal teenage 'huh!' that Sophia Loren wasn't too bad, either.

I kept an eye out for Italian movies from that moment on. Whether it was a home-grown classic, such as *La Dolce Vita*, or one of the Hollywood variety, such as *Roman Holiday*, there seemed to be one incontrovertible truth: all a guy had to do to look cool was jump on a Vespa and buzz down to a café, a beach or glamorous nightclub. No matter the time of day or night, there would always be a clutch of beautiful women with large, dangerously pointy breasts waiting to flirt with him. And once he threw his leg over a Vespa, even with a three-day growth and crumpled suit he was nonchalant style personified. To a young guy still wearing flannelette shirts and ugh boots in the western suburbs of Sydney it was a heady revelation indeed.

So it became my dream to go to Italy and buy a

Vespa – an older one, with saddle seats and a little too much chrome. I'd ride around the countryside drinking espresso and flirting with women with curvaceous figures and dark, burning eyes. I'd live *la dolce vita*, the sweet life, like Marcello Mastroianni, in a sharp suit and Ray Bans. And, naturally, I would look – and *be* – exceedingly cool.

It remained just a dream through my teens and my twenties, when getting a degree and a job became my main priority. And in my thirties, too, although the sight of Gwyneth Paltrow and Matt Damon on a Vespa in *The Talented Mr Ripley* did have me contemplating the idea of chucking it all in and running away to Italy for a couple of weeks. But it probably would have remained for ever a dream, except for that late-night commercial for Tae Bo Gold.

Instead of ringing Mr Blanks and giving him my credit card details, I fired up my computer and went to the Google website. I typed in 'Buying a Vespa in Italy' and clicked on the Search button. Precisely 0.24 seconds later I had 1180 links to websites with information about buying a second-hand Vespa in Italy.

I could have gone to bed then, content that I had made such an impressive start on my quest. Let's face it, before the Internet came along it would have taken me months to gather even a fraction of that information. But I continued, fascinated, and to be honest a little scared of the bizarre world I had stumbled upon.

Dario in Bologna warned of unscrupulous folk passing off cheap Vietnamese copies – 'Charlies' he called them – as original Italian Vespas. Henrik Borjesan of the Netherlands warned potential buyers to be wary of rust and jumping gears. Elsewhere 'Scooter Trash' – hard-core enthusiasts who rode and repaired their own bikes – were having a good old moan about yuppies buying all the well-restored Vespas as retro accessories.

Then, just as I was about to give up and go to bed, I stumbled on a site for a Vespa workshop and museum near Pisa. There was an email contact for 'The Waspmaster' at the bottom of the page (*vespa* is the Italian word for wasp). I tapped off a quick email saying that I wanted to buy a Vespa and ride it around Italy, explaining that it had to be the same vintage as me and in approximately the same condition – a little rough around the edges but still going okay.

I got a reply almost immediately. The Waspmaster didn't have a suitable bike in his workshop, but there was a 1961 Vespa on eBay Italy, the Italian version of the Internet auction site, that I might like.

'Just digit "vespa" in the search box,' he wrote. 'It's in Milan and it looks just right.'

My Vespa inquiry on eBay Italy resulted in fifty-seven items, including an original headlight for a GS160, an oil-cap clip for a 1968 Rally, a chrome Vespa bird that the seller insisted would look lovely on the front wheel guard, and a set of 1950s postcards featuring pretty girls riding Vespas, which was fanned out in a most attractive manner. Each item had a short description and a picture.

The bike The Waspmaster had suggested was about halfway down the list. The picture was only a tiny thumbnail but I knew immediately that I had found the Vespa of my dreams. It was a pale coffee colour with two saddle seats and a fancy chrome crash bar that ran along both sides, protecting its voluptuous curves. There was a provocative flash of red on the front hubcap, but the bike wasn't shiny or sparkly. The owner had allowed it to age gracefully, keeping it clean and covered, rather than tarting it up with shallow cosmetic improvements like a spray job and a lick of tyre black. It looked dignified and elegant, a fine example of a Vespa that age.

I had never wanted something more in my life. I put in my top bid of €1260, printed off a picture of the bike, pinned it on my noticeboard and went to bed.

Five days, six hours and twenty-three minutes later I was the proud owner of a 1961 125cc Vespa with saddle seats and a little too much chrome.

All I had to do was get to Milan and pick it up.

CHAPTER ONE

Milan

Kinder Surprise Toy: Push and Roll Kangaroo Family
(K02-008)

Standing in front of Milan's huge Fascist-era railway station clutching a red vinyl bag, I felt like a Cold War spy. But I wasn't there to make a drop; rather, I was waiting to meet a guy about a Vespa. His name was Gianni, and because I'd bought the bike on eBay we'd never actually met. The bag was my way of letting him know which person milling outside the Milano Centrale railway station was me.

I'd found the bag in London, in a Mod shop down the back of Covent Garden, among pointy shoes and bomber jackets emblazoned with Union Jacks or bullseye targets. It had a large white Lonsdale logo on the side and was big enough to fit a camera, a guidebook and, at a pinch, a couple of slices of Parma ham. I had been tempted to go the full Paul Weller, with a pair of stove-pipe trousers, a sharp-cut shirt and a suitably Moddish haircut, but after a quick look at the prices I decided the bag would suffice.

Right on ten-thirty a blue Mercedes stationwagon pulled up. The driver, a bespectacled guy with thinning grey hair and a salt and pepper beard, reached across and wound down the passenger-side window. 'Tell me,' he asked in perfect English. 'How is Olivia Newton-John?'

I'd only just read an article about Livvie in a women's magazine in my dentist's waiting room a few weeks before so I was able to answer confidently that she had recovered from her breast cancer scare and had a relationship with her daughter that was more like a friend than a mother. The driver signalled for me to get into the car.

Gianni introduced himself as I buckled my seatbelt. He was nothing like I had imagined. I had pictured him as a slick Lothario who looked like Marcello Mastroianni and spent his days making love and devising ways to avoid paying tax. In reality he was more your Roman senator kind of Italian, dignified and patrician, like Derek Jacobi's character in *Gladiator*. I'm sure I was nothing like he imagined, either. The Olivia Newton-John question suggested that he'd seen *The Adventures of Priscilla, Queen of the Desert* and figured that because I lived in Sydney I was the kind of Aussie male who dressed in sequins and rode on floats in the Gay and Lesbian Mardi Gras parade.

Gianni ran an import–export business from a small office a few minutes from the railway station. The office was at the bottom of a nondescript apartment block and was overflowing with plastic items he imported from China. There were bowls and buckets mainly, but also plastic table-and-chair sets for the kiddies. Two wooden desks pushed up against each other, each with a computer and a phone, formed the nerve centre of the operation.

Gianni motioned for me to sit at one of them. Then he sat down at the desk opposite, clasped his hands in front of him and asked me what my intentions were. I felt like I was being interviewed by my future father-in-law.

I told him that I planned to ride to Rome, heading south from Milan in a haphazard manner and lingering wherever the mood took me. I'd bask in the sunny weather of late spring and early summer in Emilia-Romagna and Tuscany and arrive in the Eternal City just before it closed down for *ferragosto*, the period in the middle of August when most people take a holiday and Italy comes to a standstill. My girlfriend, Sally, who was working in London, would join me in Tuscany for two weeks in July to help me celebrate my birthday with a glass or two of one of the Super Tuscans. As plans go, I thought it was pretty cool.

Gianni listened carefully, nodding his head, and then suggested I get something bigger than a 125cc Vespa. 'If you bought a 150cc you could go on nearly every road in Italy,' he said. 'With this bike you must go on the small roads.'

I said small roads were good. They went through small towns.

He warned me that on such a small bike I would get very tired. 'A journey that usually takes two hours will take two days on this Vespa,' he said.

I had to stop myself smiling. That was *exactly* what I wanted – a bike that would force me to slow down and enjoy the countryside at an Italian pace of life. I wouldn't have any choice but to picnic beside fields of sunflowers or in the shadow of an abandoned farmhouse.

Realising he wasn't going to talk me out of it, Gianni unclasped his hands and grinned. 'I guess you'd like to see your bike, then,' he said.

The Vespa was in another part of the office, in an area that Gianni had sectioned off with corkboards and which served as a workshop for his collection of old bikes and cars. I spotted the Vespa peeking out between two partitions. It was sitting on a small mechanic's ramp with its rear cowl off and the carburettor lying in a tray alongside. Even in a disembowelled state it was beautiful, and I caught myself beaming like an idiot.

Gianni explained that he had kept it in a friend's garage for the past two years because he was running out of space.

'No fuel has gone through the engine in two years,' said Gianni. 'But it is nothing a mechanic cannot fix in two hours!'

He pointed out some rust on the body and a few bubbles on the chrome, concerned that I would be upset. 'I do not know what my friends have been doing with my Vespa,' he said. 'When I left it with them it was perfect.'

I told him not to worry. It was a forty-year-old bike that had been allowed to age gracefully. I would have been more concerned if he had tried to hide these insignificant blemishes with a dodgy spray job. This way I got all the little original touches that would have otherwise been lost. Like the sticker on the inside of the guard giving instructions on the appropriate tyre pressure for different loads. Or the diamond-shaped metal badge pop-rivetted on the front wheel guard with the details of the garage it was bought from. I loved every little bit of it.

Next we sorted out the paperwork. A number of forums I had visited on the Internet while I was researching the trip suggested that it was difficult, even impossible, for a foreigner to own and register a vehicle in Italy. There had been mention of *Escursionisti Esteri* licence plates, a form of registration for foreigners who plan to stay in Italy for two months or more. But on a trip out to the soulless Motorizzazione Civile, the motor registry, in Molino Dorino, I discovered that it was only available for new vehicles.

Gianni suggested what he called an 'Italian solution'. The bike would remain registered in his name and when I finished the trip he'd cancel the registration and export the bike to Australia. This meant I would have to trust that Gianni wouldn't call the police and report the bike stolen as soon as I rode off. Similarly, he'd be hoping I'd settle any parking fines I might run up.

The Italian solution also resolved the issue of insurance. Only the day before I had made tentative inquiries about insurance at SARA, the state-run insurance company, on the pretext that the bike would be kept in Gianni's name. I wanted to know if I'd be covered as the rider of what was effectively somebody else's bike. I'd seen one too many insurance ads, where a hapless driver parks his car and forgets to put the handbrake on. He invariably finds it in a ditch a couple of kilometres away, having got there by way of a greengrocer's, a china shop and the lounge room of a local priest, who just happens to be serving tea to a group of parishioners.

The SARA office was behind Piazza Castello, an area of handsome boulevards, stately apartments and expensive shops, and it had an imposing entrance, complete with a doorman, that seemed more appropriate for a swish hotel than a state-run insurance company. I was ushered up a grand flight of marble stairs to see Laura, an elegant blonde who sat at her desk in an immaculately tailored suit, her glasses pushed up on top of her head in a manner that suggested she was about to lunch at an expensive restaurant rather than flog an insurance policy.

I explained my situation and asked if I would be covered if I bought insurance in the name of the man I was buying a Vespa from.

She nodded sagely as I spoke, then, after a short silence, looked me straight in the eye. 'If Mario Rossi insures the bike,' she pronounced solemnly, 'anyone can ride it.'

Mario Rossi. I repeated the name, hoping she would tell me who on earth he was. When she didn't, I cautiously asked how things would proceed.

'It's very simple,' she said. 'You bring in Mario Rossi's paperwork, fill in the form, pay the money and the insurance is issued in Mario Rossi's name.'

She said it all with such surety that I knew Mario Rossi, that, hell, everyone knew Mario Rossi, I was hesitant to admit that I didn't. It even crossed my mind momentarily that he may have been the local Mafia don. But I knew that if I didn't ask, I'd spend the rest of the day trying to find him.

'Ummm,' I said hesitantly. 'I don't actually *know* Mario Rossi.'

'Mario Rossi is just an example,' she tutted, giving me a withering look. 'Just bring in the paperwork of *your* Mario Rossi.'

'You mean Gianni?' I asked gamely.

'If that is his name, yes,' she said, exasperated. 'Gianni, Mario, it doesn't matter. The fact is, whoever insures the bike you can ride it.'

I left SARA reassured that I could ride the bike and, God forbid, if anything did happen I'd be covered. And greengrocers, china shop proprietors and local priests across Italy could breathe a hell of a lot easier.

With the bike sighted and the Italian solution agreed upon I handed over the €1200 (Gianni had knocked €60 off the price in a show of good faith) and the deal was done. There was one hitch, though. Gianni had lost the original registration papers and needed to get new ones issued before I could take the bike.

He assured me that getting new papers was not a big deal. It simply meant visiting a police station for a document that declared that the papers were lost and then a quick trip to a motor registry or one of its sub-agencies to have the papers re-issued. Gianni asked if I wanted to come along and I happily said yes. I was keen to see Italian bureaucracy at work.

The decision was made to go on Gianni's scooter. It was quicker in the heavy Milanese traffic and easier to park.

Gianni tossed me one of his spare helmets and pointed to a Honda parked outside his office.

'Shouldn't you be riding an Italian bike?' I asked, a little shocked.

Gianni smiled benignly and answered my question by pushing the ignition button. The bike purred to life instantaneously. 'Ahh Honda,' he said with an ironic grin. 'She goes first time.'

Gianni chose to visit the police station in Greco-Turk, an exclusive suburb of large villas with manicured gardens and tall trees surrounded by high walls. It wasn't the nearest police station – but it was a rich area with very little crime. 'It will be quicker because there will be less people,' he said, smiling. I was obviously in the hands of an expert, someone who had done this many times before.

At the Greco-Turk police station Gianni bounded up the stairs and beckoned for me to follow. We were in a race against the clock now. Government offices closed between 1 and 3.30 pm for a daily siesta, and as it was already past noon we were in danger of having to come back after lunch. Gianni hoped to sort the insurance out then and still have time to take the bike to his mechanic mate, Bruno.

The bored girl at reception directed us to the *Ufficio Denunce* at the other end of the corridor. Apparently Gianni had to 'denounce' his lost paperwork. It sounded a bit Jerry Springer to me but Gianni assured me that all he had to do was get a form, fill it in and have it stamped. We stood outside the *Ufficio Denunce*, milling behind a woman who was obviously first in the queue. Shortly after, an old couple came along and milled behind us. All the while a policeman who looked an awful lot like Ed Harris sat behind his desk shuffling paper.

'Time here is nothing,' whispered Gianni, as we listened to the wall clock tick. 'You can spend thirty seconds or four hours and it is the same. My friend says it is the only place you can taste eternity.'

Eventually Ed Harris looked up from his paperwork and asked, '*Primero*?' (who is first?). The woman before us went in and was quickly dealt with. Gianni followed and, after explaining our situation, was given a form to fill in. It was a *Dichiarazione di Smarrimento* (a declaration that something is lost) and consisted of the usual stuff like name, address, age and not quite enough space to tell your sorry tale. As Gianni filled it in I passed the time flicking through six large albums full of mug shots of wanted criminals – to help with denunciations, I guessed. They were thuggish-looking men, mostly, thick-set blokes with tattoos and low-set brows, but there were a few bookish types who I fancifully imagined were student revolutionaries.

'I hope I never see your photo in there,' said Gianni, looking up from the form.

As we waited for the form to be approved and stamped, an old guy with a mop and bucket came into the office. He had various trigger-release cleaning products strapped to his belt, pretty much like the Italian police have their guns strapped to theirs. When the Ed Harris look-alike didn't jump up immediately to let him clean under the desk, the old guy got cranky and took his time mopping the office. Then, out of spite, he wouldn't let Ed back in until the floor was completely dry. On getting permission to return to his desk, Ed tippy-toed across the room, being careful not to get it dirty. The old cleaner watched, scowling, his window cleaner drawn like a gun, his finger on the trigger ready to squirt the cop if he slipped up.

I asked Gianni why the cleaner didn't wait fifteen minutes and clean the office when everyone was on siesta.

Gianni turned, looked at me incredulously and asked, 'When would he have his siesta?'

Siestas are one of the cornerstones of Italian life, along with football, the Pope and changing your government every seven months. The word siesta originates from the Latin word *sexta*, referring to the sixth hour or midday, and has come to mean taking a couple of hours off in the middle of the day to go home for a meal and a nap. Italians will tell you that it makes them more productive workers – by having a nap at lunchtime they avoid the mid-afternoon sleepiness that afflicts workers in other parts of the world. But in the short time I'd been in Italy I'd dealt with some pretty dozy folk after three in the afternoon and I suspected that siesta was really an extended lunch dressed up as tradition. But hey, good luck to them for having pulled it off.

Gianni's form was stamped and the new document issued at 12.57 pm. It was too late to sort out insurance so Gianni suggested we have lunch. We headed back into the traffic, even heavier now that Milan's workers were rushing home for their nap. As we rode along, Gianni took the opportunity to give me some advice on handling Italian traffic.

'There are certain phrases you must learn for driving in Italy,' he yelled over his shoulder, cutting in on the inside of a large lorry. 'One is *bastardo* and the other is *vaffanculo*.'

Vaffanculo means 'fuck you'. And Italy's highest court of appeal had recently ruled that obscene phrases like it had become so common in heated arguments between motorists that they were no longer to be considered a crime against honour.

'Very useful for when you are speaking to a policeman,' I said.

'Obviously,' said Gianni, turning, with a grin.

We came to a crossroads on one of Milan's main boulevards, and witnessed an accident between an Alfa and a van. As if to illustrate Gianni's linguistic lesson the Chinese van driver waved his arm at the Alfa driver and yelled '*Vaffanculo!*'

'See!' said Gianni, pleased with the turn of events. 'He is Chinese but he knows what to say!'

Gianni chose a restaurant at the bottom of an apartment block in a down-at-heel neighbourhood. It had outdoor tables that overlooked a scruffy park with a children's playground.

When he parked the scooter on the footpath, right next to the restaurant, I asked him if it was legal.

'There is the law, and there is intelligence,' Gianni said sagely.

I pressed him on the matter and he said that while, strictly speaking, it is illegal to park on the footpath, as long as you weren't blocking anything important, like the doors to a hospital emergency room, for example, the police usually turned a blind eye.

The restaurant certainly wasn't going to win any restaurant design awards. The waitress was grumpy and the view of scruffy guys drinking from brown paper bags in the park opposite was not as picturesque as others I've seen. But if the meals being served to the patrons were anything to go by, the portions were generous and the food beautifully presented.

This was normal, according to Gianni. 'Even in a place like this,' he said, waving his arm expansively over the faded tables and torn tablecloths, 'the chef takes great pride in the food he presents.'

Gianni expanded on his theme. Food was a central part of Italian culture and based on *campanilismo*, a profound sense of locality. The men and women who prepared it were passionate about preserving local cuisine.

Perhaps this was why, when I looked at the menu, I didn't recognise anything from Italian menus back home. Panicked, I had gone for a rather boring pasta, but now I was staring at a plate of thinly sliced, cured raw beef, arranged in a circle around the plate with olive oil and a squeeze of lemon, that the ill-tempered old woman had laid before Gianni. He said it was *bresaola*, a dish only found in Milan. It looked absolutely delicious.

'Would you like some?' he said after noticing I was staring.

I nodded, drooling, and thinking he was going to give me a slice off his own plate. Instead he waved the waitress over and ordered a plate for me as well. 'If you cannot finish it, I will help you,' he said.

One slice and I knew there was no chance of that happening.

As we ate Gianni told me that I would be only the third owner of the Vespa. He'd bought the bike from the original owner thirteen years earlier. 'His name was Giorgio,' he said. 'He is dead now, but his wife, Valentina, lives in a retirement home near Genova.'

According to Gianni, the Vespa had played an important role in bringing the couple together. Giorgio had bought the bike especially to take Valentina dancing and had loaded it up with all the accessories to impress upon her father that he was a man of means. There was the chrome footrest that doubled as a protector on the cowls, and the red hubcaps with the spiffy playing-card symbols. It had a chrome bumper at the front, genuine Vespa floor mats for the running boards and a two-tone vinyl cover for the spare wheel with a zip-up pocket for maps. There wasn't much else that could have been accessorised.

Realising he needed to impress Valentina as well, Giorgio had installed a second saddle seat, with springs that gave it extra bouncy comfort. In Italy in the sixties courting a girl was a long and drawn-out process. He didn't want Valentina turning him down because she was saddlesore.

Apparently, on the first Sunday of every month, after church and still in their best clothes, Giorgio and Valentina would go to Pavia for lunch. They would ride beside the canal until they came to a small restaurant by the water that was famous for its *rana*, frog's legs, a local delicacy. After a year of lunching on frog's legs, Giorgio asked Valentina to marry him and she agreed. The Vespa, decked in white ribbons and flowers, was used as their wedding vehicle. I realised then that I wasn't just buying a bike. I was being entrusted with a piece of Italian social history.

We finished lunch with a Kinder Surprise, the chocolate eggs with a toy inside that are a distinctly Italian treat. There was a box full of them beside the cash register, with pictures of the toys inside, all displayed at jaunty angles that screamed 'crazy fun!' Among them was a green Vespa, a tiny replica of the model Gregory Peck and Audrey Hepburn rode in the Hollywood classic *Roman Holiday*. Gianni was convinced that one of the eggs would contain a Vespa. Instead, he got a kangaroo that took some putting together but, once you did, rolled its eyes when you pulled its tail. I got a bizarre creature in the shape of a teapot. The chocolate wasn't that great – it has an after-taste of Nutella – but from that moment on I was determined to find a Kinder Surprise Vespa before my trip was over.

The traffic had grown even heavier and noisier since lunch, indicating that siesta was nearly over and the good folk of Milan were returning to their offices. Gianni fired up the Honda and we made our way to a branch of the Automobile Club di Milano in yet another suburb.

In Italy, the various autoclubs operate as branches of the motor registry department. To the untrained eye they look like just another travel agency. But behind the glossy posters of the Taj Mahal and the Pyramids of Giza is a trained professional who can sort out your rego, sell you insurance and suggest a very affordable seven-day package to the Costa del Sol.

And just as with police stations, Gianni had a particular autoclub branch he preferred to visit. Or, to be precise, a particular female autoclub employee. 'She is a miracle worker with documents!' he said with a grin that suggested that wasn't all she was a miracle worker with.

When we walked into the office Gianni's friend was harshly chastising another staff member, but when she spotted Gianni she blushed and broke into a girlish smile. Her name was Maria and Gianni flirted with her, telling her my story in English.

She showed off by replying in English. 'You only visit me when you have problems!' she said with a mock pout.

Officially it takes six weeks for new registration papers to be issued, even with the proper paperwork from the police. But this was Italy and Maria told Gianni if he promised to take her out for lunch she would issue them straight away. He turned to me, shrugged his shoulders and agreed.

Maria had the papers done in ten minutes, sorting out the insurance and signing me up with the road rescue service of the Automobile Club d'Italia (ACI) at the same time. 'It will cost you €50 but it will save you hundreds,' she said. 'If you break down they will come to you. If it can't be fixed they will take it to the nearest mechanic.'

It was just before four by the time all the paperwork was done. The finer details of Gianni's lunch date with Maria were arranged. Bruno, Gianni's mechanic mate, would be fixing the few little things that needed to be done on the bike that afternoon.

Gianni dropped me back at Milano Centrale and told me to meet him in the same spot at noon the next day. 'Bring your bags!' he yelled before darting off into the traffic on his Honda.

Almost immediately a driver tried to cut him off.

'*Vaffanculo*!' I heard him shout. And he waved his arm wildly.

CHAPTER TWO

Lake Como

Kinder Surprise Toy: Viking Sailboat
(K02-070)

By eight o'clock the next morning the temperature
had already hit 32 degrees Celsius. The weather fore-
casters were tipping a top of 39 degrees, saying it was the
start of a heatwave that would last a week. In the centre
of town the normally ultra-cool Milanese were looking
flustered, removing their designer sunglasses to mop their
sweaty brows. Hot and bothered tourists in the plaza
around the cathedral were eating ice cream for breakfast
in an attempt to cool down. Yet from the roof of the
cathedral, through a forest of white stone spires and a
heat haze generated by the plaza below, I could just make
out the Alps in the distance, still covered in snow.

I'd ventured into the historic centre of Milan to tick off a few of the city's sights before setting off on my grand adventure. I'd been so caught up in the legalities of buying my Vespa that apart from a brisk stroll through the Sforzesco Castle and a quick lap around the cathedral I hadn't really seen much of Milan at all. Not that there was an awful lot to see. As a major munitions centre, Milan had been flattened during World War II. The Allies spared the historic centre, but that was about it. For the eager tourist all that was left was the Duomo, with its 135 spires, the Galleria Vittorio Emmanuele II, a perversely ornate shopping arcade with a stunning glass ceiling and mosaic floors that made the Queen Victoria Building in Sydney look distinctly like trailer trash and, north of the plaza, the Golden Quadrangle, a parallelogram of streets where all the top designers had set up shop.

As I wasn't exactly in the market for an €1800 necktie, I had a quick browse and was back at my hotel to check out by eleven. The manager seemed sad to see me go – after only two days I'd become his longest-staying foreign guest. He invited me to share one last espresso and pastry with him.

I was excited and jittery about taking possession of my bike and left for the railway station soon after, getting there a whole twenty-five minutes early. I passed the time by texting Sally in London, telling her how wonderful it would be when she got to Italy. A few minutes later she texted me back. 'So the bike goes okay, then?' she queried. I realised with a rising sense of panic that I had never even heard the bike's engine ticking, let alone seen it moving.

I'd been caught up in my dream and had forgotten to follow even the most basic rules of buying a second-hand vehicle. If I'd been back home I would have had a REVs check to see if there was any outstanding finance on the vehicle. And I certainly would have insisted on taking it for a spin. But here, in a foreign country where they spoke a different language and I would have no chance whatsoever of explaining anything to the appropriate consumer watchdog, I had blithely handed over €1200 on the vague promise that the Vespa in pieces in front of me would be running and roadworthy within twenty-four hours. I paced backwards and forwards, slapping my forehead at my stupidity. My behaviour made the nearby security guard skittish – I'm sure he thought I was one of the mad homeless people that usually hung around the fountain – and he fingered the gun in his holster nervously.

Gianni must have telepathically sensed my concern, because he arrived right on noon, not in his blue Mercedes stationwagon, but on my bike. It cut a handsome form among the taxis and the hire cars as he pulled up beside me, revving the engine exaggeratedly.

There was a huge grin on his face. 'She goes like a rocket,' he said. The wattage of his smile made me suspect that this was a turn of events not totally expected.

I excitedly put my bag on the rack, securing it with octopus straps, and climbed on behind Gianni. Then we set off into the Milan traffic. The bike struggled a bit at first – it was over forty and was powered by a tiny 125cc engine, after all – but after blowing a bit of blue smoke it perked up, and soon we were weaving in and out of cars, dodging trams and ignoring lights. Peeking around Gianni's shoulder, with the wind in my face, I felt exhilarated.

Bruno the mechanic had fixed the carburettor, put a new bulb in the front light and attached a side mirror on the right-hand side of the handlebar. Gianni said I probably could have got away without a mirror because originally my Vespa didn't have one. But now, with a mirror, the police would have no excuse to pull me over.

Gianni had also bought me a lock and chain and a litre of oil to keep in the side panel. I'd need to put the oil in the petrol. The 1961 Vespa has an old two-stroke engine and you have to add the oil manually every time you fill up with petrol. It's not the most environmentally friendly way to power a vehicle. But it's extraordinary how much power it squeezes out of something that is really just a glorified sewing-machine engine.

We stopped at a petrol station on the way back to Gianni's office to fill up with fuel. Petrol stations in Italy still have attendants, blokes in greasy overalls who fill your tank, check the air in your tyres and wash your windscreen, if you have one. The attendant at this particular station was convinced I had to put in 5 per cent oil and snorted at Gianni's suggestion that I put in 2 per cent. In the end I compromised and put in 3 per cent. Clearly my rusty maths skills were going to get quite a work-out over the next couple of months.

We arrived at Gianni's office and I loaded my bags onto the Vespa. The waterproof motorcycle bag that held most of my belongings sat heavily on the rear luggage rack. And my red bag with my camera and guidebooks sat snugly in a gap between the front rack and the leg shield. I was trying to keep the front rack free for when Sally arrived with her bag, but even without her bag the bike already looked like a Nepalese Sherpa off to climb Everest. It didn't seem to affect its performance too much, though. I rode it up and down the street out the front for a while, getting the feel of it and adjusting to the hand-controlled gearshift.

On most motorcycles you change gears with a foot pedal, but on a Vespa you pull in the clutch on the left-hand side of the handlebar and turn the handle itself at the same time to go through the gears. After twenty minutes I felt like I had the hang of it and signalled to Gianni that I was ready to go. After years of dreaming and a few months of scheming my forty-year-old Vespa was loaded, fuelled up and, most importantly, still going. Gianni jumped on his Honda and told me to follow him. He was going to direct me to the road to Lake Como.

I hadn't planned to go to Lake Como. It was north of Milan, whereas my ultimate destination – Rome – was to the south. Gianni, however, felt that the relatively short 70-kilometre journey represented an ideal opportunity to get to know my bike better and iron out any practical considerations I may have overlooked. And should any niggling mechanical problems pop up – although he was quick to point out that by rights they shouldn't – I could bring the bike back to Milan and get them fixed immediately. There may also have been a little bit of national pride involved. Gianni regarded Lake Como as one of the most beautiful places in the world and would consider it a travesty if I didn't see the place for myself.

In case I needed any more convincing, he assured me that it would be much cooler up on the lake. 'It is where we Milanese go to escape the heat,' he said. With a heat-wave on the way that was not an unimportant consideration.

As good a plan as it was – and it was an excellent one – it was still contingent on me getting past the T-intersection at the bottom of Gianni's street. It wasn't the most dangerous intersection in Milan, but it was still daunting, involving a hair-raising turn onto a major road, cutting across oncoming traffic to a lane on the far side. I couldn't see a break in the traffic, but Gianni zipped off on his Honda, darting through a split-second gap and pulling over to the side of the road a couple of hundred metres away. He waved for me to follow, but I sat, waiting patiently for a safe break that never came. Gianni waved again, frustrated, before magically doing a U-turn through a seemingly endless stream of traffic and coming back to me. 'You must not have fear,' he shouted through his helmet. 'If they see you they will not hit you.'

As if to prove the point he did the same right-hand turn again, squeezing through a gap as a truck was bearing down on him. I waited a few seconds before following, my eyes nearly closed and my body tensing for the inevitable collision. Miraculously, when I opened my eyes again I was on the other side of the road and puttering along. Trucks and cars and other scooters darted around me, but there were no horn blasts or aggressive shouts of *vaffanculo*. I had made my first foray into Italian traffic and survived.

I pulled up beside Gianni at the first set of lights, grinning with pride.

'*Bellissimo!*' he said. 'Remember: when you ride like you own the road you *do* own the road!'

We rode together past soulless apartment blocks and drive-thru McDonald's restaurants until we reached an industrial area that was as uninspiring as the ones back home. Here Gianni pulled over and pointed to the *strada provinciale*, the B-road, that headed north to Como. 'If you keep going straight,' he said, 'you will eventually get there.'

I was surprised to feel a dull sadness in the pit of my stomach. Somewhere deep inside I guess I had hoped Gianni would join me. At the heart of his dry witticisms there was always a useful nugget of information, so I'm sure he would have made the journey to Como less daunting.

I said goodbye and thanked Gianni for his help. He shrugged his shoulders as if it was nothing, and sat on his Honda and watched me wobble north. When I brought the bike back under control and looked in my side mirror, Gianni was waving and shaking his head. My grand adventure had begun.

The northern suburbs of Milan are not the most attractive part of Italy. It is a land of warehouses and factories and the workshops of truck mechanics and tyre merchants who service them. Any homes that still stood were long abandoned and are now covered in black grime. The road was potholed and bumpy, and on that hot, sticky Saturday afternoon in May, the only sign of life was the guard dogs panting heavily as they patrolled factory compounds surrounded by chainwire fences. This was not what I expected the backroads of Italy to be like. I'd expected men in cloth caps, not guys in faded blue overalls covered in grease.

Twenty minutes to the north I negotiated a huge roundabout and then giant mega-malls began to appear. It had never occurred to me that Italians might shop in mega-malls. I had imagined them visiting a number of local shops, picking up a tomato here and a slab of mozzarella there and chatting to the local shopkeepers for all the local gossip as they popped their purchases into a woven bag. But here, on the outskirts of Milan, they were pushing fully laden shopping carts across a huge asphalt carpark just like their cousins in America. The only sign that I was in Italy and not Idaho was that the patrons were more stylishly dressed than your average North American Wal-Mart shopper.

The proximity of Milan ensured that not all the malls were selling bulk-buy boxes of Weetbix. Some of the fashion houses had factory outlets here, too, where you could pick up a lovely little Versace or Dolce & Gabbana outfit at 70 per cent off. They don't like you knowing about the outlets' existence but, according to Gianni, who was surprisingly up-to-date on such matters, Posh and Becks *always* pop up to the factory outlets whenever they're in Milan.

As tempting as it was to pick up an Armani suit knocked down to a bargain price I rode on. The malls soon gave way to pleasant towns full of villas set behind mossy walls and surrounded by luxuriant gardens and parks with fountains and statues that would be museum pieces back home. This was where Milan's wealthy industrialists lived, close enough to commute to work, but far enough away to escape the noise and pollution. Not long after I was approaching the outskirts of Como.

Lake Como is near the Swiss border and sits hard against the Alps. It is shaped like an inverted 'Y' and was formed at the end of the last ice age, when a glacier melted and the basin it left beneath the Grigna Mountains filled with water. As a result, the lush, green mountains that surround the lake rise immediately and sharply from the shore. It is quite unlike any other lake I have ever seen. Como is tucked at the bottom of the Y's left arm, with the mountains stretching away to the north, lining the lake and dotted with the red-tiled roofs of villas. That day only the closest were visible. The rest were a smudge of blue, cloaked by a haze created by the heat.

Como is famous for its cathedral – perhaps the finest example of the transition between Gothic and Renaissance styles – and as the birthplace of Alessandro Volta, the guy who invented batteries and the man I hold ultimately responsible for the TV ads featuring that annoying 'Never Say Die' Energizer battery. I planned to stop there, maybe even stay overnight. But I spotted a road lined with rhododendrons and azaleas that curled alluringly up a wooded hill, and I followed that instead.

I was on my way to Menaggio, apparently. The lake lay picturesquely on my right and the air was thick with the overwhelming aroma of honeysuckle. This was what I had hoped touring Italy by Vespa would be like. I could smell the smells. I could hear the sounds. I could feel the sun on my skin. I wasn't in a car with a windscreen between me and the world outside. The villas, painted mustard or terracotta, the manicured gardens, littered with statues and sculptures, even the lorry carrying Kinder Surprises in front of me, were all close enough to touch. When a seaplane banked overhead and landed with a graceful splash on the lake just to my right I let out a sigh of contentment that could be heard over the whine of my bike's tiny two-stroke engine.

The road north of Como was a varied one. Sometimes it sat high above the lake, going through tunnels kilometres long that were drilled through the side of the mountain. At other times it dipped back down towards the water, passing through tiny villages that had barely changed in centuries. Here the road was just a tarmac version of the tracks that ran through these villages in medieval times, barely wide enough for an oxen-pulled dray, let alone the delivery lorries that insisted on using it now. So when I came into Argegno and found a lorry wedged between two buildings on either side of the road, I was not surprised. Not that it overly affected my journey. I simply followed the lead of the other scooter riders and mounted the footpath to get around it.

The further north I ventured the prettier the scenery

became. The aristocracy from Milan has been escaping to Lake Como for centuries, leaving its mark in the form of elegant summer houses and beautifully manicured gardens. When the temperature rises the Italian masses have always preferred to go to the coast, so the lakeside has been mercifully spared the blocks of ugly concrete flats that go hand-in-hand with mass tourism. It has changed so little that I could still see what had inspired composer Franz Liszt to write the Dante Symphonies, his homage to Dante and Beatrice, here. Or why Benito Mussolini lingered one extra night during his attempted escape to Switzerland. It proved to be Mussolini's downfall – a gang of partisans came calling for him that night – but I'm sure he kept that spectacular view in his mind as they dragged him back to Rome to face the music.

The youth hostel in Menaggio is one of the most beautifully situated in Europe, sitting on a hill above the road with views over the lake and the town. My arrival caused quite a stir. As I rode up the hill and approached the stone driveway, the bike backfired loudly and stuttered to a stop. The other guests, many enjoying the late afternoon sun on sun loungers, looked up, startled from their books, and the kitchen staff rushed out in their stained aprons, convinced that a gun had been fired. When they realised it was just some fool on an old motor scooter they went back to what they were doing.

The manager, a young guy called Alberto, with a

goatee and long brown hair, strode over with his arms wide open. I thought he was going to hug me but he walked straight past me and slowly circled my Vespa instead.

'It is *beauuu-tiful*,' he said, shaking his head. 'It is rare to see one so old.'

Alberto asked me where I had bought it and when I told him my story and what I planned to do, he insisted that the rest of the staff come back out to look at my Vespa.

One of them was Dave, a stocky mechanic from Melbourne with a shaved head, who was working as the hostel's chef. He had heard the bike backfire and suggested that it might be a fuel blockage. 'Could be a problem with the lines; could be rust in the petrol tank,' he said. 'You never know with an old bike like this.'

At that moment, almost as if on cue, Gianni rang my mobile to see how my first day on the road had been. He was disturbed to hear that the bike had backfired and conked out. 'It could be the choke,' he said. 'Take the filter off and stick your finger in the hole. If that doesn't fix it I'll come up to the lake and get you.'

I pushed the bike into the hostel compound, parked her under a willow tree, and decided to look at the problem the next day. It was still pushing 30 degrees Celsius and what I needed was an ice-cold beer, a long hot shower and a good night's sleep. My crash course in Vespa Mechanics 101 could wait until the morning.

I am not very mechanically minded. As a teenager I pulled the lawnmower apart to see how it worked. After discovering that mechanics was as unfathomable as trigonometry, I tried to put the mower back together again, only to find, in horror, that I now had a pile of seemingly unrelated bits. My dad had to buy a new mower, paid for from my pocket money over the next couple of years.

My mechanical incompetency used to disturb me. I felt that stripping an engine and putting it back together again was something I should innately be able to do. Just as a woman knows exactly what make-up suits her best and how to apply it expertly, I should have known which end of a spark plug went where. Then I saw my sister's attempt at Cleopatra-style eyeliner and I learned to live with my shortcomings.

Shortcomings aside, I knew that if I was to attempt to ride from Milan to Rome on a forty-year-old Vespa I would need to have at least a basic understanding of how a 125cc two-stroke engine works. That's why one of the first things I did when I won the auction for the Vespa on eBay Italy was buy the Haynes

Owners Workshop Manual for that particular model.

Haynes owners workshop manuals are reassuringly old-fashioned relics of a time when there was more to tuning your car's engine than hooking it up to a computer. Even the company logo, a book surrounded by a laurel wreath, looks like it was designed in the 1950s. The manuals are full of badly photographed mechanical procedures and amazingly intricate exploding line drawings of engine parts, right down to the tiniest of screws. They give refreshingly forthright instructions like 'Connect the rubber hose to the stub of the air cleaner box', and pepper them with practical advice like 'Make sure the hose is not kinked or split'. I spent much of the flight from Australia reading and memorising mine, lulled by its straightforward language into thinking that pulling out the flywheel to adjust the points was something I was more than capable of doing.

So it was with a certain degree of confidence that I pulled off the engine side cowl the next morning. I removed the air filter as Gianni had suggested, and then flicked through the manual, trying to match what was in front of me with one of the pictures. Upon finding one that almost looked right, I stared at it, trying to divine a hole that might benefit from my finger being stuck in it.

I must have looked quite pathetic because Dave wandered over to watch. 'Yep, staring at the manual,' said Dave, with a grin. 'That's going to fix it!'

I ignored his sarcasm and began an exploratory grope around what was left of the air filter.

Dave told me to be careful with the rubber bits. 'They look cheap to replace, but they're not!' he offered knowledgeably.

I found the hole Gianni was talking about. It was the air intake valve for the carburettor. If you're impressed that I know that, don't be. Dave told me as I stuck my finger in and forced it open. I put the air filter back on, making sure it was not cracked or kinked, and getting covered in grease and oil in the process. For a split second I almost looked authentic, but then the screwdriver I was awkwardly holding spontaneously fell out of my hand and any shred of mechanical competency vanished.

'Ever thought of taking up the trade?' asked Dave, as I lost a screw for the fourth time. 'You're a natural.'

I ignored his jibes and replaced the cowl. After wiping my hands I kicked the start lever, and after a few goes it started. It spluttered a little at first but after I revved it a few times it idled smoothly.

I think Dave was as surprised as I was. 'Like I said,' he grinned. 'You're a natural!'

I jumped on the bike and rode off down the hill, back towards Tremezzo. Tremezzo is a beautiful lakeside village famous for its annual Asparagus Festival and the imposing Grand Hotel. Built in 1910, the Grand Hotel is five storeys high, with 100 windows facing the lake. Its outside dining areas recall a time when Milan's glitterati frequented the place, their red, open-topped Alfas parked carelessly in the carpark opposite.

Of late Tremezzo has become famous with hard-core sci-fi freaks because it's where you get the boat to Villa Balbianello, the place where a rather mawkish love scene was shot between Padme and Anakin Skywalker in *Star Wars II, Attack of the Clones*. The movie wasn't that successful, and the love scene shot there even less appreciated, so the expected flood of Star Wars fans never eventuated, which I'm sure even the shopkeepers of Tremezzo would agree is not a bad thing.

There was an oversized LED temperature gauge over the door of the *farmacia* in Tremezzo and as I passed I noticed with alarm that it was 44 degrees Celsius. I hadn't really felt the heat – on the ride down from Menaggio there had been a constant cooling breeze on my skin – but when the bike spluttered and backfired and came to a stop in front of a stall selling tacky knick-knacks like a Lake Como souvenir ashtray and a faded Ferrari flag, I suddenly felt very hot indeed.

The road was narrow here, made even narrower by the tour buses that periodically squeezed through, so I pushed the bike back to the carpark in front of the Grand Hotel. There, in front of well-to-do guests taking their morning breakfast at iron tables under bright umbrellas, I attempted to start my Vespa. It quickly became apparent that kick-starting wasn't going to work. I'd have to clutch-start it.

There is no elegant way to clutch-start a Vespa, particularly in a heatwave and *especially* while you're being watched by the staff and guests of one of Europe's most exclusive hotels. I ran up and down that tiny strip of tarmac, getting the bike to an acceptable speed before letting the clutch out, hoping that would turn the engine over and spark it to life. After a dozen attempts the best I got was a screech from the tyres as they skidded and gripped.

Eventually I gave up and pushed the bike the 4 kilometres back to Menaggio. The road that had seemed so scenic the day before was just a big hill now, and sweat gushed from every pore. I must have looked quite a sight because a young couple kissing fervently on a park bench beside the lake stopped what they were doing to watch me pass.

Dave was waiting at the gate of the hostel to greet me. 'Oh, you went for a swim!' he laughed, pointing to my shirt drenched in sweat and clinging to my skin. 'I thought you might have broken down!'

Gianni called that afternoon and I told him what had happened. Within two hours he was at the hostel, and after a quick look at the bike, he decided to take her back to Milan.

'Bruno will rebuild your Vespa,' he said as Dave and I helped him lift it into the back of his Mercedes. Then, pointing to the two Italian women sunbaking topless in the garden of the villa across the way, he suggested that it was best that I stay up in Menaggio. 'The scenery is much better here than in Milan!' he said with a wink. 'I will call you when your bike is ready.'

'He really didn't have to do that,' said Dave as Gianni drove off. 'Once you paid your money and rode away it really wasn't his problem any more.'

He was right. In normal circumstances my bike would be down at the mechanic's shop in Menaggio, with the mechanic rubbing his hands together at the prospect of how much money he could milk from a silly foreigner on an old Vespa. Instead, my bike was on her way back to Bruno in Milan, who would fix whatever was wrong. When everything was as it should be, I would get the call. Until then, I would have to kick back on Lake Como, in a pretty little town with some rather racy inhabitants. Life can be cruel sometimes.

Although my Vespa was back in Milan, her influence up on the lake lingered. The story of how I had acquired her, my plans to ride to Rome, even the story of Gianni coming up from Milan to collect her when she broke down acquired instant legend status in the hostel. Every night at the bar Alberto would ask if I had heard about my bike and when I said I hadn't he'd slip me a free beer as a form of commiseration. I was also allowed to hang out in the hostel during the day (all the other guests were kicked out between 11 am and 3 pm) and when the hostel was full one night (a group of Germans had booked it out months before) I was allowed to sleep in the staff quarters for free.

My story was just as well known down in the town. On one of my first days in Menaggio Dave took me to the Internet café in the local library. He introduced me to the librarian and told him my story. The librarian was a friendly guy with tousled hair in his late twenties, and after that, whenever I went to the library to check my email, he asked how the bike was.

It turned out he too once owned a Vespa. 'It was when I was a student,' he told me one day. 'The *olio*. You say oil? It was always a problem.'

On one of my visits I met his wife and young son. His wife couldn't speak English, but we were introduced anyway. After we shook hands the librarian told her my story in Italian. I heard *Australiano*, Vespa and *vecchio* and watched as she *ahhed*! and nodded her head.

When he'd finished she said something and indicated for him to translate it to me. 'My wife wants me to tell you our Vespa story,' he said a little sheepishly. 'On our first outing – you say date? – well, my Vespa she breaks down. I tried to fix it but I got *olio* everywhere, even on her dress. At first she was angry but when she saw me sad and dirty, she forgive. She says that she knew then that she would marry me.'

When the librarian finished, his wife held his hand and smiled at him. Everyone in Italy, it seemed, had their lives touched by a Vespa, in one way or another.

Massimo, who owned the Free Time Bar, the little restaurant-bar on the small alley that ran between the library and the main square, knew my story too. Dave had taken me there for a beer after Gianni took my bike away and had filled him in on my sorry tale. Massimo had big, sad eyes and whenever he asked after my bike I thought he was going to burst into tears. It could have been that business was slow. The heat had driven most of the customers away, and the few that he had sat at the bar drinking coffee and watching World Cup soccer matches on the television above the espresso machine.

'You should come here on Saturday,' he said to me on one visit. 'Italy is playing South Korea for a place in the quarter finals.'

I did. Italy lost and the customers Massimo had counted on staying to celebrate disappeared into the night. Ten minutes after the game the bar was deserted and Massimo shut up and went home himself.

There was a lot to like about Menaggio. With its red-roofed buildings and handsome square it would have been a pretty place even without its stunning lake-side locale. When it was warm and balmy it felt like a summer holiday town anywhere. But when you walked along the boulevard with its flower boxes full of geraniums, past teenage boys and girls laughing and flirting and looking stylish in Armani, you could be nowhere else but Italy.

But it was the little incongruous corners of Menaggio I liked most. Like the Mini Putt Putt Golf Course. The Mini Putt Putt Golf Course was a crumbling collection of painted concrete traps. The attached kiosk sold beer and didn't mind if you took it on the course with you. And it was right beside the lake, which was nice, especially at night, when you could look up from your shot to admire the twinkling lights of houses scattered up the mountains on the opposite shore.

And so the days passed. Breakfasting on yoghurt and home-made fig jam on the hostel terrace. Walking up the mountain to the *rifugio* for a spectacular view over the town and the lake. Cycling to the markets down at Lenno and noting with satisfaction that Italians are drawn to the same crappy plastic items and cheap polyester clothes as the rest of us. Ice-cold beers at the Free Time with sad-eyed Massimo. The *passeggiata* down at Lago Luna, where the pretty girls on holidays from Milan walked by hand in hand. The late-night calls to Sally in London, telling her that I wished she was there.

I spent close to a week in Menaggio and by the end of

it there wasn't a gelato scooper or a ferry ticket seller who didn't know my story. They'd practise their English by asking if I'd heard anything about my bike, slipping me an extra scoop of gelato or giving me a return for the price of a single when I told them I hadn't. One night I went down to see a band playing at the Lido with Dave and total strangers came up and asked me about the Vespa. I felt like I'd become part of the community, an integral character in the town's rich fabric.

It couldn't last, of course, and on Monday evening I got a call from Gianni. 'Your bike is fixed,' he said. 'Now come to Milan and take it the hell out of my office!'

To be honest I was disappointed that it was ready so soon. I had come to like Menaggio. A lot.

CHAPTER THREE

Broni

Kinder Surprise Toy: Spider with Ladybird
(K02-075)

When I returned to Milan I found my bike on a sheet of plastic in the middle of Gianni's office. The engine cowl was on the floor beside it and Gianni was making some last-minute adjustments. When he had finished he put the cowl back on and wheeled the bike out onto the road in front of his office. With great delight he kick-started her first go. He stood revving the bike with a smile on his face, waiting for me to be impressed too. I was.

'The intake valve in the carburettor wasn't opening and closing,' he said, as if I knew what he was talking about. 'You won't have any more problems now.'

I took the ring road to the south of the city where the S35 headed to Pavia, one of northern Italy's most important cities during the Middle Ages. There were more direct ways to get onto the S35, back through the historic centre and out through Porta Ludovica. But to my mind that way offered countless opportunities for getting horribly lost. If I stuck to the ring road I was guaranteed to hit the turnoff. And if I went in an anti-clockwise direction I could turn on to the road south to Pavia without crossing lanes of traffic coming in the opposite direction.

My ride around the ring road went remarkably smoothly, so much so that I briefly entertained the idea of pulling off at Piazza Santa Maria delle Grazie to see Leonardo da Vinci's *Last Supper*. It's painted on the wall of the refectory there, having miraculously survived a direct hit in World War II, but I quickly abandoned that plan just as the turnoff approached and I found myself trapped in the middle lane between a truck on one side and a van on the other. I learnt from the experience, though, and spent the rest of my journey on the ring road in the outside lane, poised to peel off when the turnoff to Pavia appeared.

I was pleased to discover that the S35 ran parallel to the canal heading south. This was where Giorgio, the first owner of my Vespa, had taken his girlfriend, Valentina, to eat frog's legs. The canal remained just to my right all the way to Pavia. I would have liked to have stopped at a small shack and eaten frog's legs, too, but Gianni had told me the canal was now polluted and the frogs were long gone.

On the outskirts of Milan the canal was full of sludge and abandoned scooters. But the further I rode from Milan, the mechanic shops and houses thinned and the canal became wider and cleaner. Soon it ran through fields of fresh-cut lucerne. The aroma of the hay and the warmth of the sun on my skin convinced me that there was no better way to be travelling through the Italian countryside.

I was happy on this minor road. It was straight and in good condition and the bugs that mashed into my shirt seemed a small price to pay for the tranquillity. It was seldom that I passed other vehicles – they were all hurtling along the freeway – and although I was travelling pretty much as fast as my Vespa would go, it didn't feel rushed. I could soak up the sights around me at my leisure – the tractors in the fields, the occasional fisherman trying his luck in the canal. Seeing the anglers with their long thin poles and canvas seats raised my hopes that the small frog restaurants might be still there. But the tiny shacks that once housed them were shuttered and abandoned.

About 8 kilometres before Pavia I passed the turnoff for Certosa, the Charterhouse, a monastery regarded as Lombardy's best example of Renaissance architecture. Built over a period of 200 years and famous for its altarpiece by Perugino, it is still home to an order of Carthusian monks who adhere to a strict code of silence. The inner child in me wanted to see if I could make them speak, just like the scene in Monty Python's *Life of Brian*, where the guy who'd made a vow of silence wouldn't shut up once he'd been made to accidentally break it. But before I could get up to those kinds of shenanigans I needed to find a room.

Well, that was the plan. The good folk of Pavia, however, seemed to have other ideas. Once I hit the outskirts of their town they appeared in packs – in Fiats, Alfas, and on all kinds of motor scooters – buzzing around me like flies, cutting me off and distracting me with their flamboyant driving. I was concentrating so hard that I mistakenly ended up on a ring road and was in danger of missing the town altogether.

The moment I realised this, the bike started playing up, too. It stuttered and popped, only half-heartedly accelerating when I twisted the throttle. As I waited at one set of lights it stopped altogether, forcing me to jump off and desperately try to kick-start it while the light was still red. When the light turned green, it still resolutely refused to start. Now the drivers who had been initially amused by my attempts to kick-start an old bike lost their patience and started honking their horns and yelling abuse at me in Italian.

I decided to try to clutch-start the bike, pushing it to a jogging pace and then letting the clutch out. The first couple of times it didn't work, the back tyre skidding use-lessly. But at the third attempt the engine violently kicked in and the bike careered off, bucking like a bronco, with me running beside it, desperately hanging on to the handlebar. I finally jumped on, and turned into a side street to bring it under control. After a couple of hundred metres I brought it to a stop, gasping for breath, and revved the engine to stop it from cutting out again.

The side street I found myself on was *a senso unico*, one way, so I followed it to the end, where I was forced to turn down another one-way street – then another, and another, and another, until I found myself in the middle of an apartment block complex. I asked a group of kids kicking a football the way back to the centre and they pointed back down the one-way streets I'd just come from. I pressed on, passing through more apartment blocks, until I was out in the countryside. Eventually I came upon a road with a sign pointing to Pavia, and ten minutes later I was back on the ring road and at a major intersection with a sign saying '*centro*'. Trouble was, there were signs for Milano, Piacenza, Cremona and Genova as well.

Now, Italian road signs are rarely very helpful. They are blue with white writing and only come in two forms: one with a destination name and an arrow pointing left, and the other with a destination name and an arrow pointing right. This is fine when you come to a T-intersection, because left or right is the only choice you have to make. But at a crossroads like this one, with a couple of roads going off diagonally as well, the system can be found a little wanting. Rather than making a sign with an arrow pointing straight or at a 45-degree angle, several of these standard signs are simply arranged at slightly different angles on a single pole. Like the political system, Gianni had joked – left and right but adjusted to suit.

The lights changed, so I quickly chose the road to which I thought the *centro* sign was pointing and moved off. A few minutes later, instead of passing the Ponte Coperto, a Renaissance covered bridge that straddles the River Ticino, or the medieval *broletto* (town hall) or any other monument of Pavia's golden age, I found myself back in farmland, passing a tractor showroom and heading towards Piacenza.

I contemplated turning around but the incident had left me so shaken I decided to keep going. I needed petrol, too, so I turned into the first road on my right, hoping it would take me to a small village and a petrol station. The road took me across a long iron bridge over the River Po, which wound through vast flats of sand and pebble. On the other side was Albaredo Arnaboldi, a small agricultural town of silos and barns, with a café and, thankfully, a petrol station, on its dusty main road.

I say Albaredo Arnaboldi had a petrol station but really it was little more than two pumps in front of a tiny shack. It was run by a little old man who emerged rubbing his eyes and hitching up his overalls. He smiled when he spotted my Vespa, and he walked around it slowly, chuckling. He asked me a question in Italian and I answered by telling him I was Australian, which made him chuckle more. As he filled up the tank I watched the bowser, trying to figure out in my head how much oil I'd have to put in. The little old guy must have noticed my pained expression because he went back to his shack and emerged with a small measuring cup with markings on the side. Apparently you filled it with oil to the mark corresponding to the amount you put in – in this case, 3 litres – and that was the right amount of oil to put in. It was ingenious!

I thanked the old guy and waved, hoping he would retire to his shack and allow me to go through the difficult process of starting the bike. But in a small town like Albaredo Arnaboldi, the arrival of a foreigner on a forty-year-old Vespa wasn't something you see every day and this guy was keen to milk as much entertainment as he could out of it. He sat on the dusty concrete ledge in front of the bowser watching, sometimes offering advice but, more often than not, simply chuckling. After ten or so attempts to kick-start the bike I decided to clutch-start it, running off down the hill and waiting until I hit the tarmac before letting out the clutch. The bike coughed and then, at the final second, spluttered to life and I was on my way again. I looked in the mirror and the old guy was shaking his head and laughing.

The sun was getting low in the sky now, casting a golden glow on the fields of hay. The air was thicker with midges and bugs, too, so I kept an eye out for somewhere to stay. For the first 10 kilometres or so I passed through flat farmland, silos and sheds the only buildings around. I figured that, at a stretch, one of those would do – a kindly farmer was sure to let me bunk down in a haystack. Then ahead I saw a hill, covered in grapevines, and a small town below it. The Vespa gods were smiling on me. A quaint town in wine country – was there any better place to spend the first night of my big trip south?

But what town was it? I hadn't noted any famous wine-producing town in my guidebook when I had checked it at the petrol station. And the encyclopedia of wine I had browsed through before leaving Australia hadn't mentioned that the area south of Pavia was a major wine-producing area.

Then I reached the outskirts of the town and saw the sign. 'Welcome to Broni – home to the Fiamberti Vineyard, fine makers of spumante.'

As a teenager growing up in Australia in the 1970s, spumante was my introduction to wine. Asti spumante was the alco-pop of my generation. It was sweet and fizzy and at $2 for a 750-millilitre bottle, it represented extraordinary value when you wanted to write yourself off. After a few glasses of the stuff my mates and I would guffaw about the fact that spumante's makers chose to advertise the drink's effect so openly via its name. Until, of course, the stuff kicked in and we were laughing on the other side of a toilet bowl.

I guess it's just unfortunate that with over one million different wines available in Italy (yes, one million!), it was the cheap stuff – the lambruscos, the spumantes and the bottles of chianti in little raffia baskets – that the Italian wineries were shipping off to the rest of the world. So, unlike sophisticated Italian teenagers, who had been enjoying a glass of wine with their meals from the moment they stopped breastfeeding, I had developed a taste for a sugary wine which gave you a hangover that kicked like a mule.

But even as a teenage aficionado of spumante I had never heard of Broni. Apparently the Fiambertis have been making wine for centuries. They even have letters from medieval popes testifying how good their wine is. But when, on the outskirts of town, I spread out my huge Michelin map, there was nothing to draw my eye to the little dot south of Pavia that marked Broni. The nearest green squiggly line – Michelin's way of marking a scenic spot – was the bridge over the River Po near Albaredo Arnaboldi.

Yet as I puttered up the high street I found Broni quite an agreeable place. The afternoon sun shone pleasantly on the centre of town, where I found a handsome square, a church with a slender bell tower, and a busy market-place with a medieval shopping arcade, called a *loggia*, with arched doorways. All the while a series of hills covered in vines formed a picturesque backdrop. On one of the quaint side streets I found a modest one-star hotel, Albergo Bedo, with shuttered windows and flower boxes overflowing with pink geraniums.

The Bedo was also a restaurant, and when I rang the bell on the counter in reception the manager emerged from the kitchen in a blood-stained apron. He wiped his hands on his apron to take my passport, and looked perplexed when he saw that I was Australian.

'Not *Milano*?' he said, pointing to my Vespa with its Milanese number plates parked just outside the door.

I told him my story about buying the Vespa on the Internet and my plan to ride it to Rome and he gave me a hearty slap on the back. '*Fantastico*!' he said.

With that he took back the key he had given me, replacing it on its hook in the little wooden key box, and gave me another. On the way to my room, he pointed out the room he was going to give me, a tiny shoebox at the top of the stairs. He screwed up his nose at it, and when we passed a room where a group of Muslim men were praying he screwed up his nose again. Then he led me down the corridor to a double room. The window had its own flower box, and looked out over the town to the vine-covered hills beyond.

'*Bella vista*!' he said proudly. He had given me the room with the best view. Travelling on a 1961 Vespa, even a temperamental one like mine, certainly had its advantages.

The sun was sitting low in the sky so I decided to go for a ride to see the sights of Broni while there was still light. I rode back through the town and down a dirt road that followed a small river into the hills. Grapevines grew in rows right up to the road. They were planted here on the steepest parts of the hills so that they got the sun for most of the day, essential for the types of grapes grown here in the Oltrepò area – croatina, barbera, uva rara, riesling, moscato and pinot (it's amazing the detail they put in tourist brochures these days). They were small vineyards, and the rough, steep paths between the vines indicated that the grapes were picked by hand.

Nestled at the bottom of one hill was a small chapel dedicated to the Madonna of the River Friar. The spot was once a popular resting place for folk walking from outlying areas to the markets in Broni. One day an apparition of the Madonna appeared to one thirsty shopper, and a statue of the Madonna was erected to mark the event. Now the statue and its battered metal donation box sat behind a locked grille. Even in rural Italy, vandalism and theft are a problem.

After tossing a few coins in the donation box, I continued along the road, coming upon a crumbling farmhouse that was so fantastically decrepit I had to stop and take a photo. I had barely brought my bike to a stop before I was surrounded by a pack of mongrel dogs, snarling and snapping at my heels and at the bike's tyres.

A rough-looking man resembling Ernest Borgnine before he shaved in the morning came to a window on the second floor, rubbing his eyes. Obviously he had been woken by the commotion. His huge belly was barely constrained by a grubby white singlet. He yelled something at the dogs, which made them stop barking immediately, and beckoned for me to come up.

Chastised by their owner, the dogs ceased growling and led me to the back of the crumbling house and a rickety staircase that climbed to the top floor. The house was falling in on itself, with huge chunks of plaster lying in crumbled piles on the floor, exposing the beams above. Oceans of rising damp had eaten away at the walls, and hornets' nests hung from each corner.

An old Vespa 125U leant against a wall, gathering dust. It was probably the reason the guy had called me up. Vespas had been popular with farmers. Ones like the 125U came with a metal parcel rack instead of a passenger seat, and at a time when the financial outlay for a truck, even a small one, was prohibitive, a Vespa with a crate on the back was a realistic alternative.

Mr Grubby Singlet had retreated to a small room that contained a single bed and a cooker. The way he shook my hand and dragged me in made me suspect he didn't get many visitors. Given the state of his room I felt I could say with some certainty that he hadn't been entertaining any ladies there lately. The sheets on the bed were torn and as grubby as his singlet and the cooker was covered in grease.

He moved a pile of dirty dishes from an old chair and motioned for me to sit down.

I wasn't really sure what was going to happen next. I couldn't speak much Italian. And he couldn't speak any English. But with the help of a phrase book I was able to determine that his name was Roberto, he lived alone and that he worked in the fields in the hills behind us. On mention of the fields he pulled out a green wine bottle and two dusty glasses. He blew the dust from the glasses and poured a shot of white wine in each. It was surprisingly good and I 'hmmmed' appreciatively, which seemed to please him. Then he remembered something and after throwing clothes, newspapers and muddy farming equipment aside, produced a chunk of ham on a plate. He carved two chunks off, offering me the biggest and greasiest.

It's always a dilemma as to what to do in these circumstances. It was generous of him to offer me a portion of his dinner. But I was certain the meat was rancid – he had cut off a smaller piece and flicked it towards his dogs and they'd taken one sniff and raced out of the room yelping.

I took the chunk he offered me and smiled, uncertainly. Then the €2 I'd dropped into Mary's donation box down the road must have kicked in, because just as I was about to risk dysentery, or worse, the dogs started fighting out on the landing, kicking up dust and causing quite a commotion. When Roberto left the room to yell at them and break up the fight I took the opportunity to flick the meat out the window.

Roberto returned and I made a show of wiping my mouth then thanked him for his hospitality. When I made my excuses to leave he gave me a greasy handshake and a hug, a charade that suggested that if I was ever by this way again I should drop in.

As I jumped on my bike I spotted the chunk of meat lying in the middle of the road, and noticed with alarm that there was a dead bird beside it. The bird may have been there first, but I couldn't be sure.

I ate in the restaurant attached to the hotel that night. I had intended to venture into the centre of town to check out some of the bars I had noticed in my earlier wanderings, but the manager's wife had other plans. She spoke passable English and was determined to practise it on me. She led me to a table in a quiet corner, away from the television, which was showing a World Cup match that nobody was interested in now Italy had been eliminated. The only other guests, six men of Middle-Eastern appearance, sat at a long table, drinking from soft-drink bottles and breaking up food they had bought at a local supermarket.

'*Rifugiati*,' she said, nodding towards them. Refugees. The local government paid money to the hotel to let them stay while their applications were being processed.

Like all the meals I had had in Italy, dinner that night came in three parts. There was an *antipasto*, a 'pre-meal' of olives and thin slices of Parma ham. Then a *primo piatto*, or first course, of pasta or risotto (in this case spaghetti with asparagus). And finally a *secondo piatto*, a second course, consisting of grilled pork. The food was simple and delicious, but each time the manager's wife brought me a dish she would ask me more about my plans and where I intended to go. As a result, the food was always cold when I finally got to eat it.

By the time I finished the meal, the asylum seekers had retired to their room and the manager and his wife had joined me at the table with a bottle of the local spumante. It was a generous gesture, but I was worried that the taste would bring back horrible memories of all those teenage asti-induced hangovers. But it didn't. It was lightly bubbled, fragrant and had a dry sweetness that was a caseload away from the sickly sweet wines of my youth.

As we drank the manager bemoaned having to work

in the kitchen in the hot weather – '*Molto caldo,*' he said. With that topic of conversation exhausted I asked them about the history of the town, and was told that apart from a few plagues nothing much happened here in Broni. Just as our conversation – and the spumante – was in danger of drying up, the manager's wife looked me in the eye and asked me if I had given my Vespa a name.

The thought had never crossed my mind. I've never been one for naming vehicles. My mum is. She names her cars before the registration papers have been transferred. She had Buttercup, the yellow Toyota Corona stationwagon, and Morrie the Magna, and her current car is Connie the Cressida. But I had never been motivated to give any of my vehicles a name. It was always *the* Datsun or *the* Suzuki, mostly with an expletive-riddled prefix added. I had never dignified a vehicle that I owned with a name.

'You should call it Sophia,' the manager's wife said. 'When I was a girl I called my Vespa Sophia after Sophia Loren. She was my high-spirited friend, making me do things I was otherwise too timid to do.'

I thought about it, and although I was opening myself up to a ribbing from my mum after all the grief I gave her about naming her vehicles, I agreed. After all, it was the old black and white movies of Sophia Loren that had inspired me to do this trip in the first place.

'For luck, with your journey,' the manager's wife said raising her glass.

We all clinked glasses, and I hesitated before taking a sip. 'To Sophia,' I said.

'To Sophia,' they replied with gusto.

CHAPTER FOUR

Ponte dell'Olio

Kinder Surprise Toy: Rolling Armadillo
(K02-002)

Although Sophia had only acquired her name the night before, I was surprised how quickly she took on the appropriate temperament. When I attempted to start her that morning, she did so with a reluctance reminiscent of a woman happily dozing in bed and it was only after giving her a little choke, the motor scooter equivalent of a shot of espresso, that she finally perked up. Ten minutes later she was still limbering up, stretching and getting ready for the day. The intermittent backfiring I put down to early-morning yawns.

I was so pleased by my chance detour to Broni I had decided to avoid major towns and major roads altogether. My immediate destination was Cinque Terre, a series of quaint seaside villages on the Ligurian coast, and the original plan had been to get there via Piacenza and Parma. It was the logical route to take. The roads were well maintained and there were large towns sensibly distanced apart should anything go wrong. The formidable Apennine Mountains, which stood between the Po Valley and the coast, were traversed by the S62, from all accounts a fine road that tamed the mountains.

After perusing my maps, however, I had decided on a more audacious plan. I would head directly south from Broni along narrow, squiggly roads. The folk back at Michelin had traced many of them with a green line, indicating they were picturesque, and they passed through little-visited, small towns like Nibbiano and Bobbio, before popping out on the west coast somewhere around Sestri Levante. That most of the area was shaded a mountainous green on the map had escaped my attention, as did numerous passes at over 1200 metres above sea level. In my mind I was simply making sure I'd enjoy the same chance encounters with friendly locals that had marked my stay in Broni.

My new plan started well enough. There was a slight delay when I was pulled over by a policeman to allow a funeral procession to pass on the main street of Broni. And I spent the first couple of kilometres sneezing from the incense a black-robed priest had been swinging in a burner as he led the parade. But the frazzling heat of the previous weeks had been replaced by the kind of heat that tickles your skin rather than fries it, and the sky was blue instead of a heat-haze grey.

I travelled along tiny roads past vast fields of lucerne. Huge combine harvesters wove dexterously around abandoned stone farmhouses and stands of trees and the smell of cut hay lingered fragrantly in the air. The only downsides were the swarms of bugs stirred into flight by the harvesters and the occasional tractor around a blind bend.

I was in Emilia-Romagna now, a province on the edge of the Po Plains that was touted as the 'new Tuscany'. Stretching from the Adriatic Coast in the east to within 50 kilometres of the west coast, it is one of the most productive agricultural regions in Italy. With that has come a strong emphasis on culinary arts and the creation of two of the country's most famous staples – Parmesan cheese and Parma ham. If you ever wondered how Parma ham gets its distinctive taste, apparently it's because the farmers feed the pigs the whey byproducts of Parmesan cheese.

In Emilia-Romagna pigs outnumber humans, and that morning I entertained the fantasy that I was alone in this porcine-heavy region, observing the rhythms of an agricultural Italy that other tourists don't see. And if they do, their hermetically sealed, airconditioned cabins rob them of the smells, the touch and even the mashed bugs that made the journey one that stimulated all the senses. Sophia seemed to be enjoying it, too, and she purred along contentedly in the mid-morning sun.

Travel agents make a big deal about finding the new version of an old favourite. Prague is supposed to be the new Paris, and Vietnam the new Thailand. But that morning the comparison of Emilia-Romagna with Tuscany didn't seem that far-fetched. Within the first hour I passed more tilled fields, more giant wheels of hay and more quaint stone farmhouses than you'd see in a Frances Mayes desktop diary.

I stopped for lunch in Bobbio, a vision of golden stone and red terracotta nestled in the Trebbia Valley at the foothills of the Apennine Mountains, then made my way towards the road heading south towards the S45, a B-road that links Piacenza and Genova. But before I reached it Sophia spluttered and coughed and then stopped altogether.

My initial fear was that the fuel line was blocked, clogged by muck that had been swilling around in the bottom of the tank. Using my trusty Haynes manual as my guide I loosened the appropriate fuel pipes and sucked on them. At first nothing happened so I sucked harder. When I got a mouthful of fuel I put it back together again. Then I tried kick-starting the bike but it stubbornly refused to start.

My antics caught the attention of an old man in a baggy grey suit and the kind of moustache favoured by

1920s silent movie stars, who was sitting on a railing beside the road, catching his breath. I asked him where I'd find the local *meccanico* and he pointed back up the road towards Bobbio, holding his arm up for what seemed an eternity to make sure I knew in just which direction he meant. In the early days when I was planning this trip I had imagined there'd be a cloth-capped mechanic well versed in the inner workings of an old Vespa in every town and village. The reality was they were few and far between.

Noticing my frustration, and doubtless my ineptitude, the old guy lowered his arm and indicated for me to step aside. With a few deft turns he pulled out the spark plug and poured a small amount of petrol into the hole. He dexterously screwed the spark plug back in and attached the lead just as nimbly. Then he motioned for me to kick-start the bike and, to my delight, Sophia fired up immediately.

I thanked him and set off, busily making a mental note of the procedure should I need to call upon it again.

Within a hundred metres or so I could tell that Sophia was still running roughly. She backfired a couple of times and grumbled if I turned the throttle too far. The sensible thing would have been to turn back to Bobbio. I could have nursed the bike there and had a proper mechanic look her over while I found a room and ate in an agreeable restaurant. But I decided to press on towards the coast, turning left down a road that was more an F-road than a B. I had no idea where I was going. The coast was still a good 150 kilometres away and the towns along the road I chose to take were represented by dots on my map that were smaller and more insignificant than the one used for Bobbio.

Sophia struggled across a series of low wooded hills to Ferriere, a rather unlovely town on the River Nure. It had a surprisingly large number of tall concrete apartment blocks that reminded me of the commuter suburbs on the edge of Milan.

I didn't spot any hotels among the apartment blocks so I decided to press on, reasoning that I might find a small *agriturismo* in the wild mountains above the town. *Agriturismi* are working farms that rent out spare rooms in the farmhouse and feed you on their produce. They are becoming increasingly popular in Italy – and commercialised, it has to be said – and offer a chance to revel in the tranquillity of rural Italy. I also had an ulterior motive. I figured that a farmer used to stripping down and rebuilding tractors would know a thing or two about sorting out a temperamental forty-year-old Vespa.

Sensing what lay ahead, Sophia backfired and stuttered petulantly. She reluctantly struggled for 13 kilometres up a steep mountain of switchbacks and forests, before giving up the ghost only a kilometre short of Passo Zovallo, one of the highest passes in the

Apennines, at 1405 metres above sea level. It was just too steep and she had had enough.

I removed the engine cowl and began my routines. I checked the fuel lines. I took out the spark plug and cleaned it with a small wire brush. I scooped a tiny bit of fuel out of the tank and put it in the spark plug hole. I didn't know what I was doing or why I was doing it – the routines were more talismanic than knowledgable. So I wasn't really surprised when none of them worked and Sophia refused to start. I decided to coast back down the mountain to Ferriere. It had seemed big enough, and ugly enough, to support a mechanic.

The ride back down the mountain to Ferriere was the most exhilarating of my trip so far. I didn't wear my helmet – I hadn't seen another vehicle since leaving Ferriere, let alone the local highway patrol, the *carabinieri* – and the engine was off so all I heard was the whoosh of the wind in my face and the sounds of the forests around me. When I scooted over streams and trickling waterfalls I felt the temperature drop, and now the exhaust was gone, the rich smells of earth and wood became even more pungent. As I whizzed through Gambaro and Selva, tiny farming communities that consisted of two or three houses, the farmers looked up from their fields, and children playing beside the road yelled and waved and ran after me. I was back in Ferriere and pulling into the tiny petrol stand in under fifteen minutes, a quarter of the time it had taken me to go the other way.

The bored attendant said the nearest mechanic was in Farini, 13 kilometres away.

Then I remembered I was a card-carrying member of the Automobile Club d'Italia (ACI), and I called the nationwide toll-free number from a public phone booth. I was put through to an English-speaking operator, who took down my details. There was nothing to do but wait.

It is a universal truth that roadside assistance any-where in the world will take at least an hour to get to you. I have long suspected that the mechanics sit around in a room somewhere, reading newspapers and drinking tea, and then fifty-five minutes after you call, they put their newspapers down, bid a hearty farewell to their fellow assistants and set off to find their stricken motorist. But even by those standards, the ACI were taking their time.

A red and blue ACI tow-truck showed up just after four. The driver, who introduced himself as Giuseppe, didn't ask what was wrong with Sophia. He just pushed her up the ramp at the back and secured her to the right-hand track with a single strap. The bike looked ridiculously small, taking up a fraction of the space that a car normally would. After checking with a quick tug that Sophia was secure, Giuseppe motioned for me to jump in the cabin and we were on our way. He couldn't speak English so I wasn't exactly sure where we were heading. All I know was that we headed north out of Ferriere, driving in a manner that suggested the fate of the world rested on us getting wherever it was as quickly as possible.

We certainly weren't going to Farini. Giuseppe powered through that village without touching his brakes, ignoring the lower speed signs and alarming the residents. The road was winding and treacherous yet he threw the truck into the corners like he was Michael Schumacher. He harumphed at the road-holding ability of the truck, saying it was *grosso*, too big for the road, and indicated towards my Vespa as if to say it would be much better.

An hour after leaving Ferriere we reached a large town. I'd been so shaken by his driving that I didn't notice what it was called.

The mechanic's shop was on a side street. Giuseppe loosened the strap and wheeled Sophia into the workshop. An older mechanic, Giuseppe's father as it turned out, came over and looked at the bike. After establishing what an Australian on a Vespa with Milanese number plates was doing in the backwoods of Emilia-Romagna, both he and Giuseppe went through the routine that I had gone through at the top of the mountain. It didn't work for them either and they indicated that I would have to leave Sophia there for the night. Giuseppe's dad took me to the back of the workshop and showed me a Lambretta that was being worked on. With the help of my phrase book it became obvious that the guy who was working on that bike, their scooter expert, would be in the next morning.

I'd obviously need somewhere to spend the night so I asked in pidgin Italian if there was anywhere to stay nearby. Giuseppe's father interpreted my expansive hand gesture to mean 'Can I sleep here on the floor of the workshop?' and shook his head, saying it was too *sporco*, dirty. He would take me to a hotel after he had locked up.

We climbed into a white delivery van and Giuseppe's father drove right through the centre of town and out into farmland on the other side. Fifteen minutes later we were in a small hilltop village.

With tree-lined streets, villas, and a park with a pavilion, it looked like the sort of spa town that rich folk come to, to enjoy a mud pack. And the hotel to which Giuseppe's father took me looked definitely out of my price range. The Locanda Cacciatori looked like a country lodge, complete with glass-eyed animal heads mounted on the walls. I tried to tell Giuseppe's dad that there was some kind of mistake. This was not the sort of hotel I usually stayed in. But he wouldn't hear of it and took me inside to meet the manager.

He explained my situation, filling in the manager on my grand quest and the unfortunate state of my bike. The manager nodded, a concerned look on his face.

He shook hands with Giuseppe's dad, who wished me a good evening and went on his way. Then he grabbed a room key and beckoned me to follow.

He gave me a room at the back, with a bath and stunning views over the tilled fields. After showing me how everything worked he told me that I was in Castione, my bike was in Ponte dell'Olio, and that dinner would be served at 7 pm.

Alarmed at the salubrious surroundings, I asked him how much it was all going to cost.

'You have a credit card?' he asked. I nodded and he gave me a vague, dismissive wave of the hand that was supposed to say 'don't worry about it', but I interpreted to mean an awful amount of money.

I showered and put on clean clothes, then gingerly ventured down to the restaurant.

It was a Friday evening and well-dressed Italian couples and family groups were arriving in shiny expensive cars. They weren't the kind of folk who ate here because it was cheap and cheerful. They'd come here because it was the place to be seen. The Locanda Cacciatori was obviously *the* place to dine. I was afraid that at any moment one of the other guests would see I was an imposter and insist that I leave immediately.

I was given a table on the terrace, with a view even more Arcadian than the one from my room. A waiter came and asked me what I wanted, and when I hesitated, mentally calculating how much credit was left on my credit card, he suggested I have the house special. That consisted of a plate piled high with Parma ham, then a delicious stuffed pasta and, finally, a selection of tasty desserts.

Some time during the main meal he asked me if I'd like a bottle of wine. What the heck, I thought. I was less than a month from turning forty. The place took credit cards so I might as well live it up. My card could well be cancelled before I reached Rome, but for the moment, at least, I was going to taste a little of *la dolce vita*. Surely my bank manager would understand when I asked him to increase my credit limit.

CHAPTER FIVE

Castell'Arquato

Kinder Surprise Toy: Kitchen Pot Spy
(K02-049)

The next morning I walked down the stairs to reception with that feeling of dread some celebrities must get whenever they open a tabloid newspaper. In my case it wasn't incriminating photos of a night of drunken tabletop carousing with LA hookers that I was worried about. Rather, it was the plate of delectable stuffed pasta that had barely lingered on my lips, and the multiple desserts, each one more delicious than the last. And the beer. And the wine. And the twelve-year-old port to finish it all off that I'd ordered with an expansive wave of my arms. I realised with a groan that my time of reckoning had come. This was going to cost me. Big time.

The manager seemed intent on drawing out my suffering. He didn't look up when I approached and continued to shuffle papers behind the counter after I coughed softly to announce my presence. I felt like I had been sent to the principal's office at school. He flicked through a folder on the desk, pretending it was of great interest, not acknowledging my presence, knowing that each passing second was torturous for me. Of course, it wasn't me that would be getting six of the best that morning at the Locanda Cacciatori. It would be my credit card. But it was painful nonetheless.

The manager finally looked up and greeted me with a quiet '*buon giorno*'. He rustled through his files some more, his glasses perched on the end of his nose, and after finding my bill placed it on the counter and pushed it towards me. I was astounded when it only came to €40. Convinced he had made a mistake, I asked if it covered everything.

'*Si,*' he replied nonchalantly. It also included breakfast, and when I was finished he drove me back down to the mechanic's shop in Ponte dell'Olio.

I was equally surprised to find that Sophia was fixed and ready to go when I arrived. The problem had been the *puntini*, the points, and Giuseppe performed an elaborate series of charades to show me everything that had been done that morning. It started with the removing and cleaning of the spark plug through to the eventual discovery that the points were the problem (this part of the charade came with a very convincing 'Eureka!' facial expression). Sophia started with a relatively light kick – the first time I'd seen her start so easily since I'd bought her.

Even more surprisingly, Giuseppe only charged me €30. That price, amazingly, included picking the bike up in Ferriere the day before, a new set of points and all the work that had been done that morning. I was beginning to suspect that I was being followed by a generous benefactor who paid my bills and told folk to charge me a nominal amount so I didn't get suspicious. A Vespa fanatic, perhaps, who'd heard of my quest. But I think it was just the effect Sophia, and my story of riding her from Milan to Rome, had on people. The Italians are a crazy and romantic people who, it seemed, appreciated the inherent folly in what I was doing. That there was no tangible benefit at the end of it all only endeared me to them further.

When I was ready to set off Giuseppe and his father and mother gathered around to say *arrivederci* and wish me a *buon viaggio*.

Soon I was riding through a network of fields that were typical of this part of Italy. Most grew lucerne but occasionally I would pass a field of stunning yellow sunflowers that were so bright and cheerful-looking I couldn't help but smile.

My plan was to turn left at Ciriano and make my way to Parma, picking up the route I had intended to take before I was waylaid by Broni and my mountain adventure. But upon coming to the crossroad in the heart of Ciriano I misread the road sign and ended up on the road south to Castell'Arquato. I didn't realise my mistake until a few kilometres later, when Castell'Arquato came into view. It was a castle on top of a hill that looked for all intents and purposes like Camelot. It seemed I was meant to be heading this way, so I abandoned my plans to turn around and continued on towards the imposing stone parapets and ramparts.

Castell'Arquato was a major stopover on the Via Francigena, a medieval trail pilgrims followed on their way to Rome. They came from all parts of Europe, taking months, sometimes years, and suffering all kinds of privations, to reach their destination. They must have felt awed, as I did, when the crenellated towers of the Rocca Viscontea fortress came into view.

The pilgrims stayed in hilltop castle towns like Castell'Arquato to avoid being robbed. The massive stone forts offered them protection and a chance to rest and replenish supplies. Aware how much money these religious 'tourists' brought into the towns, city fathers actively pursued their custom, pretty much in the manner cities and countries pursue tourists today. They offered special deals to encourage pilgrims to choose their fortified city rather than the one a little further down the valley. The medieval stone gate leading into Piacenza, for example, features a stone relief from 1330 of happy men, women and children, declaring that everyone who enters will be 'welcomed and well received'. Elsewhere, churches and monasteries were built, often on the basis of dubious miracles, such as the spotting of a long-forgotten saint, in a bid to encourage pilgrims to stay a little longer.

I made my way along a road, climbing through forest that grew beside the massive stone walls, and following signs pointing to a hostel located at the top of the town. It struck me that my discovery of Castell'Arquato had the makings of a modern-day miracle too. My bills from both Locanda Cacciatori and Giuseppe reeked of divine intervention.

The hand of God was clearly evident, too, when the hostel, the Conservatorio Villaggi, turned out to be a fully restored, fourteenth-century Dominican monastery with flagstone floors, exposed beams and attached bathrooms for only € 30.

Wandering the narrow streets of Castell'Arquato I congratulated myself on discovering it. The ancient stone buildings blended seamlessly with the cobbled streets, giving the impression that very little had changed over the centuries. In Tuscany, such a quaint, picturesque town would have been overrun with tourists, daytrippers mainly, taking snapshots and stocking up on overpriced olive oil and rancid hairy boar ham. But here the only other people on the streets were locals, who viewed my habit of taking photos of buildings, fountains and squares with deep suspicion.

A bocce tournament was in progress in a carpark at the bottom of town, and with nothing better to do I found myself buying a gelato and picking out a spot on the prefabricated stand thrown up specially for the event. The white gravelly surface had been divided into two lanes about the size of a ten-pin bowling lane and a sponsor's banner was hung across both, as well as a string of foreign flags, to give the impression that the annual Castell'Arquato bocce tournament was an internationally significant event. Either that or there really were representatives from Sweden and the US trying to secure the very attractive winner's cup, which featured two naked ladies holding a bowl. It was displayed on a table in front of the lanes so competitors could see just what they were playing for.

From what I could gather bocce was a less manicured version of lawn bowls and very much a male domain. Men in matching white sports shirts with telltale creases that suggested they were fresh out of the box and bought especially for the tournament huddled in groups at either end, discussing shots and disagreeing on strategies. Like lawn bowls back home, bocce seemed to be primarily a game for blokes of a certain vintage, and their long-suffering wives were the only spectators.

I didn't stay to see who won. Instead I made my way back to the park beside the castle to watch the sun set over the hills. I dangled my legs over the stone wall, a sheer drop of 20 metres to the scrub below me, and watched the fields opposite change colour, drifting through various shades of gold, each one darker than the other.

It was now officially Saturday night, but in Castell'Arquato that amounted to little more than eating in one of the outdoor restaurants and then a quick *passeggiata* through the main square. Anyone below retirement age had headed off to the clubs in the big smoke of Piacenza, half an hour away. I wandered back up through the town towards the hostel, getting lost down tiny alleys and startling myself at the sound of my own footfall. It was only 8 pm but the town was already eerily quiet, the only sound the occasional cat-fight on a low wall or the drip of water from a tap on a terracotta tile, placed over the ancient stone to protect it from wear.

I stopped at a crossroad marked by a shrine to the Virgin Mary. Sitting on the shrine's steps, surrounded by dancing fireflies, I texted Sally.

Within seconds she texted me back. She was at the local video shop and asked if I had any ideas for her evening's viewing. I suggested any movie from the Kirsten Dunst oeuvre – *Bring It On* for something uplifting and inspiring, or perhaps *Crazy Beautiful* for something a little more thought-provoking. There was silence for a couple of minutes – a lifetime in the world of texting – before two beeps announced the arrival of a colourful message that indicated my Kirsten Dunst suggestions were not entirely appreciated.

Still, it struck me that I was living in extraordinary times. I was in a medieval town in north central Italy, sitting under the gaze of a statue of Mary that ancient pilgrims prayed to on their journey to Rome, giving real-time advice to my girlfriend in her local Blockbuster in North London about what video she should hire. A message that would have taken months to reach its destination not so long ago was received in a split second. It should have made me feel closer to Sally but instead it emphasised the distance between us. For a moment I wished I was back in London. Then another text message came through and I was happy to be where I was: Sally had ended up borrowing a George Clooney film.

I left Castell'Arquato the next morning to the sound of church bells, weaving my way through small groups of locals in their Sunday best making their way to church. I decided to stick to the Via Francigena, heading south along the same route the pilgrims had taken centuries before. It was marked by signs featuring a cartoon of a monk carrying his possessions on a stick over his shoulder, and took me through Vernasca, Bardi and Borgo, before finally coming out on the S62 at Pontremoli. It was an agreeable journey, past imposing hilltop castle towns and down mountain roads that s-bended lazily through stands of trees and past freshly shorn fields of hay. The fields were terraced by low, stone walls and were for the most part empty – the farmers were at church. The few farmers who were tilling the fields looked up from their work as we passed and, upon spotting Sophia, smiled broadly.

I loved the way Sophia had that effect on Italians. People having animated conversations in streetside cafés would stop talking to watch her pass. Petrol station attendants invariably asked how old she was. And whenever I parked her I would return to find someone admiring her with a grin. It seemed that in Italy everyone's first vehicle was a Vespa just like Sophia, and the sight of her brought back fond memories for all.

It reminded me of a story my friend David Vitiello had told me before I left Australia to do this trip. His family had moved to Australia from a small farm near the Italian–Swiss border in the 1960s. Back in Italy his father had owned a Vespa, a 150GS, and every Sunday the whole family would ride down to the village as a special treat. Once they got there they had to decide whether to buy a pizza or petrol for the ride home. If they decided on pizza they would walk home, their father pushing the bike.

Back then, shortly after World War II, Italy was not an affluent country. The Italians were a vanquished people and their country's infrastructure had been largely destroyed. Families struggled to put a meal on

the table, and petrol and transportation were expensive.
Few could afford a car. Enrico Piaggio, the chairman of
the Piaggio Company, saw the need for a cheap, reliable
form of transport for Italian families to get about on,
and set out to create a 'motor scooter for the people'.
The Vespa was born, and to Italian families in the 1950s
and 1960s a Vespa was the equivalent of a shiny four-
wheel-drive to families today.

By early afternoon I hit the S62, the *strada provinciale*
connecting Parma with Tuscany and the Liguria Coast
in the west. I had imagined it to be quite a major road –
it was marked by a thick red line on my map – but it was
an unassuming stretch of bitumen with grassy verges
dotted with tiny daisies. Furthermore, I only had to wait
for a solitary car to pass before I turned on to it.

The approach to Pontremoli was even less remarkable. It was lined with greasy mechanic's shops and
houses covered in grime that seemed to get worse
the closer I got to the town. Tucked up against the
Apennines, and beside the cascading Magra River,
this ancient town should have been lovely. It had its fair
share of handsome buildings – the Castello del
Piagnaro and the seventeenth-century cathedral were

particularly fetching – but compared to the towns of Emilia-Romagna it looked grey and grubby.

In the time of the Via Francigena, Pontremoli was the first major port of call after the perils of the Apennines. And for pilgrims heading back from Rome to their homes, it was the last stop before the hard work of crossing those mountains began. Pilgrims spoke of it as a den of thieves and greedy merchants. They called it the *clavis et lanua*, the key and the door, to the Apennines.

It seemed little had changed. Whereas Castell'Arquato radiated a golden light, Pontremoli was dark and grimy. The old stone here seemed to suffocate light and throw shadows darker and murkier than anywhere else I'd been in Italy.

I'd been riding since ten so I stopped for a coffee at a small café just off Piazza della Repubblica. I greeted the man lazily cleaning the counter and ordered a *caffè macchiato*, hoping to impress upon him that, despite appearances, I was a sophisticated chap well versed in the intricacies of Italian coffee etiquette. A *macchiato* is an espresso with a dash of milk, or a stain, as Italians quaintly put it, and is the acceptable way to have milk in your coffee in the afternoon in Italy. Cappuccino, my favoured form of coffee, is regarded as a morning drink, the milky froth considered too creamy and unsettling for delicate Italian stomachs any later.

Back in Milan Gianni had told me that ordering a cappuccino anytime after 10 am was akin to snogging a nun. When I told Gianni that I liked the frothy milk – half the fun is scooping it off and eating it, I reckon – he suggested the *macchiato*. 'There is no *spuma*,' he had said, 'but there is milk, though not enough to offend.' Gianni had also made it very clear to me that I was always to drink my coffee at the counter. Cafés charge a lot more if you sit at a table and, according to Gianni, only rich men do it. 'And with this bike,' he said, waving his arm towards Sophia with a grin, 'you will *never* be a rich man!'

I indicated to the guy in Pontremoli that I would drink my coffee at the counter, once again hoping to impress upon him that I knew exactly what I was doing. He gave me a look that I interpreted as 'Hey, I know that's the rules, but hell, there's no one here. Sit down, make yourself comfortable and I'll turn a blind eye.' It wasn't until I went to pay that I realised what he had really said was that I might think I had things sussed but he was still going to wrangle three times the normal price out of me, anyway. Five hundred years on and the merchants of Pontremoli hadn't changed one little bit.

From Pontremoli the road wound its way south beside a mountain and high above a river course. The motorway that most people used was across the valley on my right, heading straight and unchallenged at the same height through the hills and valleys and over the river below. The S62 was more circuitous and prettier, I think, but grew less and less scenic the closer I came to the coast. Aulla, for example, was a confusing conurbation of turnoffs, freeway entrances and bypasses and multiple, doubled-up road signs that pointed in seemingly different directions at once.

At one of those crossroads I was presented with three options to La Spezia, the large town at the bottom of Cinque Terre. There was no indication of a highway number for any of the options or even the number of kilometres each one involved. That I chose the one that passed through Bottagna, lightly touching the northern parts of La Spezia before putting me directly on the road to Pian di Barca and the turnoff to Cinque Terre, was more good fortune than good navigational skills.

So too was my arrival time. It was late in the afternoon and the sun was low in the sky. The sea glinted like the chrome on a Mod's Vespa and I realised that it was the first time I'd seen the ocean since I'd been in Italy. I was high on cliffs, backed by pine trees that were richly fragrant and which gave the coast an olive-green hue that was very Mediterranean. The light was clear and the sun was warm on my skin.

I couldn't imagine a lovelier time to first glimpse the rugged coast of the Ligurian Riviera.

CHAPTER SIX

Cinque Terre

Kinder Surprise Toy: Crab in a Bulldozer
(K02-056)

Back in the fifties, when less than 10 per cent of homes in Italy had electricity and running water, and eating meat was a once-a-week treat, the coast represented an escape from the hardships of everyday life. A highway was built between Milan and Rome that ran beside the sea – *l'autostrada del sole*, the sunshine motorway, as it became known – and for two weeks a year Italians would cram onto pebbly beaches and eat ice cream and go chestnut brown in the hot August sun. And more often than not it was the family Vespa that took them there.

Chances are they'd also bought the Vespa on credit.

When Piaggio had problems flogging the first fifty Vespas they came up with the idea of allowing customers to pay in instalments. Even though it was simple and cheap the price of a Vespa 125 was a little less than the entire annual salary of a blue-collar worker, and eight times the average monthly salary of a white-collar worker. With the easy-purchase plan all you had to do to take delivery of a brand new Vespa was cough up a small deposit. The rest could be paid off over a period of a year or two.

Of course, these days everyone buys a vehicle on finance. Only pop stars and lottery winners pay cash. But in the 1950s it was a radical concept. It was so radical that Piaggio was the first European company to try it and it left them so financially exposed that not only was the future of the Vespa at stake, but the future of the entire company as well. Thankfully the gamble paid off and by 1953 more than half a million Vespas had been sold.

Soon everyone was zipping around on Vespas, and despite the poor condition of the roads it seemed there was no limit to where Italians could take their 'engine-powered freedom'. With a little bit of enthusiasm, perseverance and self-sacrifice there wasn't a corner of the country that couldn't be conquered by a Vespa.

It was these audacious – and, by the sound of things, reckless – Italian families on Vespas that opened up places like the Cinque Terre. The Cinque Terre is a stretch of rocky coastline along the Riviera di Levante, named after five isolated villages that cling dramatically to the cliffs. It stretches from Monterosso al Mare in the north to Riomaggiore in the south, and it wasn't so long ago that the villages could only be reached by the sea. Even now there isn't a road that links them all together.

The whole area is protected as a designated World Heritage Area, and this, combined with the fact that the land is simply too difficult to build on, has saved the Cinque Terre from becoming overdeveloped. The five villages have changed little over the centuries, a jumble of pastel-coloured walls and terracotta roofs seemingly tumbling down the cliffs to the sea are backed by vineyards planted on terraces cut into the side of the mountains by hand. The steep path that links each village is notoriously treacherous and locals revel in telling stories of hapless tourists falling to their death on the jagged rocks below.

I had decided to stay in Vernazza, the village my guidebook strangely described as the 'most sociable' in Cinque Terre. I rode along a narrow road that snaked its way down through Mediterranean pine forest and became increasingly cluttered with parked cars the closer I came to the village. Most had Italian plates, but there were German, French and Dutch cars, too, even the odd English one. At the top of the village, still 2 kilometres from the harbour, a boomgate manned by a chap in a grubby, ill-fitting uniform stopped motorists going any further.

I rode up to the gate with a smug smile on my face and waited for the man to raise it. I was on a Vespa, after all, and an old one at that. Up until this point riding Sophia was like being given the keys to the city – or village. Free right of passage was but one of the privileges it had afforded me. But the guy just shook his head, pointed to a notice that said 'Residents Only' and indicated in an unfriendly manner that I should turn around and go away.

I was shocked. Motor scooters were usually exempt from motor vehicle restrictions. I asked the gatekeeper if he spoke English and he nodded and asked if I spoke Italian. When I said no, thinking that he would explain the situation in English he simply said, 'You are in a lot of trouble, then!' It was the first time I'd come across such a rude, brusque attitude in Italy, and it threw me.

I chained Sophia to a signpost, but I didn't like the idea of leaving her there. Not because I couldn't bear to be apart from her – it wasn't so long ago that she'd spent the night in a mechanic's shop in Ponte dell'Olio. But I was a little concerned because the sign warned against rock falls. The steel frame of your average Vespa is deceptively strong, but some of the boulders loitering on top of the cliff looked pretty big.

In summer the Commune di Vernazza kindly provides a minivan service to shuttle visitors from the boomgate to the start of the village, following a stream lined with farmhouses and in the shadow of steep hills covered in vines. It's not free – this is Italy after all – but the price of €1.50 was clearly visible on a piece of paper taped to the front window to avoid any mis-understandings. Of course, that didn't stop the driver from trying to charge me extra, 'forgetting' to give me my change when I gave him a €2 coin. Without Sophia I was regarded as just another tourist to be fleeced at will. Until that point I hadn't realised how much money she'd been saving me.

Walking into the historical centre of Vernazza is like walking onto a 1950s Italian movie set. A single path runs from the top of the town to the sea, lined by faded four-storey houses – painted yellow, terracotta and salmon, mainly – and a collection of smaller buildings that tumble down the hills behind the path on either side, all jostling for a view of the sea. Vernazza is the only village on the Cinque Terre with a natural harbour and, as if to celebrate, each side is crowned by a suitably picturesque grand building: on the left the remains of a castle; on the right, Santa Margherita d'Antiochia, a fourteenth-century church.

I couldn't find a room on the main square so I began exploring the narrow lanes, linked by steps or *arpaie*, that crawl up between the houses on the hills. Houses here climb vertically up the hills, so that you are never more than a hundred metres from the water as the crow flies. But when I knocked on the doors, the little old women in aprons who answered shook their heads, having anticipated my question of '*Camera?*' (room?).

If I'd been worried about putting on weight from eating Italian food and riding around on a Vespa (I wasn't) I reckon I lost the extra pounds that afternoon. An hour later I had searched every nook and cranny in Vernazza, backtracking down lanes and stone staircases, and even mistakenly setting off down the Sentiero Azzurro (the Blue Path) towards Monterosso, thinking that a room might be found in a farmhouse in the vineyards high above the town. In fact, I went over every square inch of the village so many times I could draw a detailed map of it even now. My search, however, threw up nothing. There wasn't a room, a bed or even a couch to spare in Vernazza.

Before throwing myself at the mercy of the minivan shuttle guy again I decided to try the rather soulless hotel that overlooked the asphalt square where the minivan disgorged passengers. I hadn't tried it before – to be honest, I had fantasised about finding a room in a house where a buxom daughter in a peasant blouse would ask me to pass her more pegs as she leaned through a shuttered window to hang out washing – and was startled to hear they only had one room left. It was a double room and if I was willing to pay the full price I could have it.

The room overlooked the railway station and I spent the night becoming intimately familiar with the timetable of Italian intercity trains as they whooshed between one tunnel and the next, just outside my window.

The next day was Monday and the weekend crowds had thinned considerably. I found an apartment above a tiny souvenir shop and for half the price I was paying at the hotel I got a kitchen, a bathroom and a fruit bowl full of inflated pink balloons. The shuttered windows overlooked the main drag and a tiny cave that led to the sea on the other side of the hill. If I lay still on the bed I could hear the sound of waves lapping through it. It was barely audible above the hubbub of the crowds and a guy with an accordion playing 'O Sole Mio'.

As I relaxed, luxuriating in the space and wondering just what the pink balloons were for, I found myself singing the old Elvis song 'It's Now or Never'. I didn't even know I was doing it at first and then I realised for the first time that 'O Sole Mio' and 'It's Now or Never' were the same song. I have since discovered that the lyrics to 'It's Now or Never' were written by Aaron Schroeder and Wally Gold, who cobbled it together in a fit of pique when Elvis insisted they write him material that sounded more like Dean Martin. For thirty-odd years I had been blissfully unaware of the connection.

Most people come to the Cinque Terre to walk along the Sentiero Azzurro, the ancient track that joins the five villages. There is a fee for walking the path, supposedly spent on maintaining it, which is collected by path wardens sitting at desks under trees or beside vineyards on the outskirts of each of the villages. Backpackers on Eurail passes get off at Monterosso railway station in the morning, walk the track in half a day and then get back on a train to continue to Rome. The less fit or the less rushed break the trip by overnighting in Vernazza or Manarola.

I did the same. But it took me close to a week to do it all. It's not that I was being lazy. During the week I stayed in Vernazza I attempted at least one section of the track each day. Some mornings I'd catch a train to a village and then walk back to Vernazza through the ancient vineyards, along craggy clifftops and past secluded bays. Other times I'd walk to a village, say Manarola, admire the riot of pastel-coloured houses there, maybe offer a few tips to the artists trying to capture the gaudiness of it all, and then catch a train back in time for my afternoon siesta. And, in my defence, I feel compelled to point out that I walked the 3.7 kilometre stretch of pathway from Vernazza to Monterosso not once, but twice!

Anyone who has walked the Sentiero Azzurro will tell you with a shake of the head that the path between Vernazza and Monterosso has more jagged peaks and troughs than a Bill Clinton polygraph test. It picks its way along clifftops dotted with jojoba plants and the occasional splash of crimson bougainvillea, and past vineyards scratched into the side of the steep hillside by hardworking Ligurian farmers. Legend of the vineyards and the strength of the men who made them reached pirates in North Africa and Corsica, who came to the Ligurian coast looking for top-quality slaves.

Of course, the renowned difficulty of the path didn't stop people who wouldn't usually walk to the post box from attempting it. As I came down a flight of rough-hewn stairs into Monterosso, an African-American woman about the size of Oprah when she's fallen off the dieting wagon threw her hands up in the air and cried, 'Lord have mercy!' When I told her that the Lord had mercy just at the top of the stairs where the path flattened out for a while, she grabbed my hand and shook it as if I had just saved her life.

Early morning was my favourite time in Vernazza. The air was fresh and clear with just a slight tang of salt. The daytrippers who came by train had not yet arrived, so the local shopkeepers used the opportunity to take delivery of fresh produce. The stock arrived on the back of tiny three-wheeled delivery vans called *Apes*, the Italian word for bees and pronounced *ar-pay*, and they buzzed up and down the main drag, calling into the butchers, the bakers and the small *alimentari* opposite my apartment. I had spotted *Apes* before in my travels, and I wondered what use such a small vehicle could have. But here in Vernazza I finally understood. They rattled down lanes and squeezed between ancient buildings and through spaces that even the tiniest pick-up truck would get wedged in. They couldn't carry much, but the proprietors of the small businesses in Vernazza didn't need much.

Down at the harbour the old women of the village took advantage of the quiet morning hours before the tourists arrived to go swimming. In those swimsuits that grandmothers like to wear, they'd float for hours, joking and laughing with each other, their words echoing around the apartments overlooking the harbour. Occasionally a friend in a building up on the hill would fling open the window of her apartment to hang out washing and the women in the water would call to her, floating on their backs as they caught up with the latest gossip.

The men of the village spent the quiet time sitting on a stone bench outside the offices of the Partito Democratico della Sinistra, a socialist political party, next to Trattoria Giani. There was a noticeboard above them, topped by a picture of a hammer and sickle on a red flag, and each morning a representative of the party would pin the pages of a left-leaning newspaper, *L'Unità*, to it. He pinned it up each morning and each morning the old blokes ignored it, leaning against the wall and stretching their gammy legs in front of them, preferring to talk about football and the price of fish rather than politics.

The first tourists to arrive were the aspiring artists

on a special-interest tour led by a semi-famous painter. Mainly ladies of a certain age in baggy cotton shirts and broad-brimmed straw hats, they set up their canvases and paints beside the harbour in the square in front of Santa Margherita d'Antiochia. They each faced different directions, pointing their easels towards the particular side of Vernazza they were trying to capture. Some looked towards the harbour and the sea, with its gaggle of brightly coloured boats moored to the sea wall. Others cast their eye over the dramatic coastline of huge rock cliffs with swirling faultlines topped by terraced vineyards. Some chose the church to be their subject. Others the tiny lanes and staircases and faded pastel houses of the village.

The painters beat the rush of tourists by a couple of hours. But to the local folk their arrival signalled the end of their time to enjoy the village. They slowly drifted off, disappearing into the warren of lanes and stairways, leaving their village to the hordes of intruders. On these mornings I felt like I was watching a TV nature programme that documented the life of a fragile species, frightened away from their natural habitat by large, aggressive intruders, and only coming out when they felt it was safe again, usually in dawn's early hours.

Having said that, the folk of Vernazza did very well out of the intruders. Before tourists discovered this little stretch of coastline, the Cinque Terre villages were depopulating rapidly. Villagers were leading a subsistence lifestyle – eating what they could catch in the sea and drinking the wine from the vines on the hills. Not that the vines were ever that abundant. Even today the region is Italy's second lowest producer of wine, after the Valle d'Aosta in the Alps, up on the Swiss border.

But the tourists came, and now, in mid-June, it was the beginning of the busy summer season. For the next three months the main street, even the tiny lanes, would be clogged with scantily clad women licking ice cream, and bare-chested men sweating profusely, and the villagers would make their money for the year. They did it by renting out rooms and apartments and by hawking Cinque Terre white wine in easy-to-carry cardboard presentation packs. They served meals at hugely inflated prices and convinced visitors that their life wouldn't be complete without a bottle of Ligurian olive oil to take home to the in-laws. They made every single sale count.

So far I had largely escaped this kind of profiteering. A man riding a 1961 Vespa from Milan to Rome was to be respected or, at the very least, afforded local prices. But with Sophia chained to a sign at the top of the town, there was nothing to set me apart from the Eurailer who had just blown in on the 10.24 from Geneva. I don't think I conducted a single transaction in Vernazza, and indeed the whole of Cinque Terre, where I wasn't short-changed.

To give the shopkeepers of Cinque Terre their due, they had a bagful of ingenious ways to exact a few extra euro cents from you. Now that I had an apartment with a kitchen and a fridge, I had taken to buying tomatoes, cucumbers, mozzarella, olives and Parma ham to make my own meals. All these items were priced according to weight, and all manner of sleight of hand was employed to up the price. One shopkeeper claimed he could weigh things just by holding them, while another thought it was perfectly acceptable to round things up (250 grams of Parma ham, for example, became 300, and one tomato became two). One wrinkly dear tried the old trick of resting her thumb on the scales to increase the weight and showed no remorse or embarrassment when I caught her out.

The most insidious ploy saw shopkeepers wrapping the items up before they weighed them. They'd carefully slice the ham, placing a slither of plastic between each slice, and then wrap it all up in butcher's paper. I know we're only talking a couple of milligrams at most, but it is milligrams of paper and plastic that I was paying for at premium Parma ham rates.

I may have been a little too militant in the pursuit of fair pricing because over the course of a week shopkeepers began to recognise me and disappear out the back when I entered the shop. Some places, like the *alimentari*, gave up trying to stitch me up altogether and charged me the same price they charged locals.

They didn't know I owned a forty-year-old Vespa. But they knew *I'd be back*.

I also befriended one of the waiters at one of the out-door restaurants. His name was Stefano and if business was a bit slow he'd pull up a seat and chat to me. One night I told him that I'd been expecting a feast of seafood in Vernazza and was disappointed to find little on the menu other than fish stew.

'Ahh, that is because the *Mare Liguria* is *molto freddo*,' he said. 'It is too cold for the fish. Any fish here, it is brought from the south.'

Except the fish in the fish stew. That was made with air-dried cod, a throwback to the times when the people from these parts were great seafarers and needed food that would keep on long voyages.

I'm guessing that they ate a lot of cod because the Cinque Terre was a little light on fresh fruit and vegetables. The local market sold asparagus, purple artichokes (*carciofi violetti*), tomatoes and some citrus fruit, but that was about it. The terraced hills above the towns were used solely to grow wine grapes or olives. At least the olives were great. They were small and dark and didn't have the bitter aftertaste most olives have.

Anxious that I was forming a bad opinion of the culinary prowess of his region, one evening Stefan asked me if I'd heard of pesto.

Sure, I said. A bit of basil, garlic, parmesan cheese

and pine nuts all mixed together. The staple of bruschetta in Italian restaurants the world over.

'We invented it!' Stefan said proudly. He pointed to the menu and I noticed that it was a little heavy with pesto dishes. There was pesto with *trenette* (the local long, flat pasta) and pesto with *trofie* (the local spiral pasta), as well as pesto on all the old favourites, such as gnocchi, spaghetti and fettuccine. The chef's special was *minestrone alla genovese* – basically a bog standard minestrone soup with a big dollop of pesto on top.

As proud as he was of pesto, Stefano was not impressed by the local white wine. It was overrated, he said. The huge demand from tourists, keen to take a souvenir of their stay in Cinque Terre, meant that quality control wasn't all it could be. In the past the wine, which is made from bosco, vermentino and arbarola grapes, was produced solely for local consumption. If it was dodgy the unimpressed locals would let the wine producer know. Now tourists were buying it as they passed through, not realising that they'd been done until they opened the wine months later when they were home again.

Stefano took a bottle from behind the bar and poured the golden liquid into two glasses – one for him and one for me. 'Try this,' he said. 'It's sciacchetrà. It's from Cinque Terra but *passito*. It is very good.'

Passito is a method of preparing a wine. Instead of immediately crushing the grapes after they are picked, they are left to dry on wooden racks, becoming raisin-like and often going mouldy in the process. The juice in the grapes condenses and becomes sweeter. The sciacchetrà was sweet, but not sickly like many German dessert wines.

For sickly sweet I had to drop in at my favourite gelateria, down by the hole in the sea wall, and get a *cono* with two scoops of *stracciatella*. It was a ritual I followed every evening after I had eaten my meal. I'd buy a gelato and then clamber out to the sea wall to watch Vernazza by night. Couples strolled through the square or ate at restaurants nearby. Kids played on the pebbly beach as their parents drank espresso. A babble of sounds would rise from the village and wash over me. Occasionally a voice would cut through, usually an American one, disconnected and yet clear like a vox pop quote. 'I asked – no, demanded – a hysterectomy,' I heard one night. 'How much is that in dollars?' was the response.

For the most part it was a soothing hum, the perfect soundtrack to the swallows darting around the harbour, cartwheeling between the church and the castle and feasting on the insects drawn to the golden glow of the floodlights. I'd lie on the stones looking up at the stars or text Sally with details of the scene before me. When I got a reply like 'You bastard!' I knew it was time to go to bed.

On my last afternoon in Vernazza I walked up to the boomgate to check on Sophia. Like most things I did in Vernazza this had become something of a daily ritual. I'd wander up the hill, gasping for breath, and sigh with relief when I saw that she was still there. I'd unchain her and start her, making sure she was going okay before setting off for a ride along the deserted roads that cut through the pine trees and hills of gorse high above the sea. I'd return refreshed and invigorated.

As I was unlocking Sophia from the pole that afternoon a lanky young American with a mop of frizzy hair approached. 'Man, is that *yours*?' he said, full of awe.

I nodded and he circled Sophia, admiring her. 'I was checking it out on my way down this morning,' he said. 'It's like full-on *Quadrophenia*, man!'

His name was Josh and he was from New York. In his teens he had been a drummer in a ska band. Ska fans were another group of people who had adopted the Vespa as their mode of transport.

'Man, we would have killed for a scooter like this!' he said. 'A few more mirrors and it'd be perfect!'

I started Sophia and he told me how, one night after a gig, they saw a really cool scooter, just like the one Sting rode in *Quadrophenia*, and the singer stole it. 'He wasn't going to keep it,' he said. 'He just wanted to ride it. But the guitarist turned him in, man, and then he had, like, the whole Mod Squad after him.' Bummer.

I gave Josh a lift up to the house he was renting with

his wife in the hills in Moro. He invited me to share some dope he'd just scrounged from some college kids heading up into France. I politely declined. My afternoon rides were for clearing my head, not clogging it. Instead, I rode along the ridge among the pine trees where the air was clean and fresh, visiting all my favourite spots: the stretch of road winding through heath that made me feel like I was in the middle of nowhere; the clifftop spot with panoramic views of Corniglia; the cool ride through the shade of a dense and pungent pine forest.

The next day I would be riding beside the Garfagnana Mountains to Lucca, a medieval town renowned for its architecture and perfectly intact city walls.

After close to a month in Italy I was going to Tuscany.

CHAPTER SEVEN

Lucca

Kinder Surprise Toy: Smurfette on a Skateboard
(K02-061)

It's funny what makes you visit one place rather than another in your travels. It's not always a picture in a brochure or a misleadingly exaggerated blurb in a guidebook. It can be a spontaneous decision to catch up again with someone you've just met. Or a half-heard snippet of information about a good bar or restaurant.

I decided to go to Lucca not because my guidebook described it as a gorgeous walled city with quaint cobbled streets, but because it had a youth hostel.

The need to watch my spending had presented itself when I checked the balance of my bank account in an Internet café on my last afternoon in Vernazza. It wasn't in bad shape. There were still funds available, which is more than could be said on previous occasions I have checked my bank balance during my travels. But if I didn't curb my expenditure I wouldn't be able to enjoy Tuscany with Sally in quite the manner I had fantasised.

You see, Sally and I had only just started going out. I was hoping that the sixteen days she spent with me in Italy would cement our relationship. Surely a few weeks in Tuscany, eating in quaint *trattorie* and strolling through world-famous art galleries would distract her sufficiently from my flaws.

It was best then, I decided, that I stayed in a hostel now than be forced to suggest it when Sally was in Italy. You can't really take a girl to a hostel. Well, not unless you want to break up with her. Even if you're lucky enough to get assigned to the same dorm, any attempt to get cosy and you'd be watched by a gallery of smelly backpackers, keen to get an eyeful of what their mates told them they'd be getting truckloads of but poor hygiene and suspect social habits had cruelly robbed them of.

And if Lucca was half as beautiful as my guidebook suggested, well, that was a bonus.

I set off from Vernazza just after eight, while the air was still crisp, and climbed up through the forested hills towards La Spezia. Because Sophia only had a 125cc engine, under the mandatory engine size required by law to use the freeways, I made the journey south from Cinque Terre by a secondary road, which travelled inland towards Lucca through the marble-producing towns of Colonnata, Cave di Fantiscritti and Carrara.

There's no way of dressing up an industry that chisels out dirty big chunks of rock from the sides of mountains. Carrara, the most famous of the towns, was a cacophony of huge trucks, giant cranes and massive diamond blades cutting slabs of marble the size of a small house into thin sheets. The marble mills and workshops create a perpetual cloud of marble dust that hangs over the town, eventually settling on everything below it, including Sophia and me. I ran my finger across the top of the headlight casing and left the kind of smudge you see in the houses of tardy housewives in ads for Mr Sheen.

There are more than 300 quarries near Carrara, and they appear like grey scars on the impressive mountains that back the town. Most date back to before the Roman empire, making the region the oldest industrial site in continuous use in the world. It's the quality of the white marble excavated here that is remarkable. Its moon-like luminescence was the stuff of legend in Roman times. Michelangelo was a regular visitor during the Renaissance. (He found the slab of stone that was to become David here, and so regular were his visits that he bought a house in Carrara's main square, just opposite the Duomo, to stay in when he was in town.) More recently, Henry Moore picked out the marble for his sculptures here.

Of course, most of the stuff cut out of the mountain these days is made into boardroom tables for CEOs to snort coke off. But in the past this was the birthplace of some of the finest and most sublime pieces of art the world has ever seen, and I'd like to think it has left the locals with an appreciation of beauty. When I stopped for petrol the young mechanic openly admired Sophia and asked how old she was. I said *quaranta anni* – forty years old – and he nodded his head, impressed. He added the oil for me, lovingly pouring it into the tank, and wouldn't let me pay for it when I gave him the money for the fuel. It was as though he felt it was the least he could do.

Just as I was approaching Lucca, Gianni rang. He hadn't heard from me for a while and was concerned I was broken down beside a road somewhere remote and he would have to come and rescue me. He seemed surprised when he heard how far I'd come.

'You have made it over the mountains?' he asked, astounded.

He was almost happy when I told him the bike had broken down and the points had been replaced. This was to be expected and he seemed relieved that it had happened. 'It was the *puntini*!' he said with a laugh. I could almost hear him slapping his head, as if to say, 'Why didn't I think of that!' He wished me luck with my journey and made me promise to call him when Sally arrived.

So with few expectations I arrived in Lucca, only to find it was a sophisticated town of immense beauty and charm. The tops of the city walls have been turned into a public park, replete with leafy, tree-lined avenues built by Marie Louise de Bourbon in the early nineteenth century. The moat that once surrounded them has been filled and is now a grassed ring of green before the inevitable circular road and new city sprawl begins. My guidebook described the walls as ramparts – squat, strong, impenetrable – and once you pass through them you get the distinct feeling that they have kept the world at bay for the last few centuries. This part of the city was unrushed and timeless and inexplicably ignored by the hordes of tourists that plague Florence and Venice. Not bad, I thought, for a cheap place to sleep.

The youth hostel was a surprise, too. It sat just inside the city walls, a large, restored and immaculately clean edifice that had once been a college for Franciscan monks attached to the impressive Church of San Frediano next door.

The dorms were at the top of an impressive marble staircase – no doubt fashioned from a white slab dug out in Carrara – and the one to which I had been assigned was full of the usual youth hostel crowd. There were young Eurailers leaning against bunks, talking about where they'd been and where they were going. And a grim Dutchman who was cycling around Europe. Plus that staple of hostels the world over, the gnarly old guy who thinks hostels should be run like repressive boarding schools and resents anyone else in the dorm who doesn't agree with him.

The obligatory old guy in this dorm was a wiry old Indian with muscles knotted so tightly around his neck he looked like he was being strangled by a vine. I got off on the wrong foot immediately by flopping onto my bed (a bottom bunk) and texting Sally. I'd turned off the sound on my phone – I realise as much as the next person just how annoying the beeps that accompany each letter are – but that didn't seem to matter to this guy. He tutted, and when I chose to keep texting regardless he came up beside my bed on the pretext of looking for something on the bunk above and farted in my face. I would have loved to have greeted him in kind but I just didn't have it in me.

Unlike a lot of walled cities in Tuscany, Lucca is flat. Flat as a pancake. And with cars largely banned from the walled city, most of the locals get about on bicycles. It gives the place a certain timeless charm, which is only enhanced by the fact that most of the locals seem to know one another and wave to each other as they pass.

The top of the city walls that surround Lucca are long (over 4 kilometres in circumference) and wide (a couple of hundred metres at least). It's a lovely place to go for a stroll and affords a rare glimpse into the immaculate formal gardens of the villas that back up against the walls. It's also a popular leisure spot at all hours of the day. In the hours just after dawn it is the domain of joggers. At sunset, it's a place where couples, both young and old, go for a romantic stroll. And at any moment you're guaranteed to find someone sitting on one of the quaint wooden benches simply watching the world go by. On my first stroll around the walls I spied an old woman sitting on a bench with binoculars and noticed with alarm that she was using them to look at me! When I got closer, however, I was pleased to see she'd fallen asleep.

And no matter what time of day there were always cyclists on the walls. They weren't the cyclists of European movies I'd imagined, either. Instead of a tweed jacket and a cloth cap these guys were wearing tight-fitting Lycra outfits that highlighted the fact they were still some way off their ideal racing weight. Although they were amateurs their tops were covered with the logos of dozens of companies, each rider choosing the shirt of his favourite team pretty much in the way most blokes buy a football shirt. (Just to give you an idea of how important the right outfit is to your average Italian cyclist, the bike shop around the corner from the hostel in Lucca devoted three-quarters of its shop space to clothing and only a quarter to actual bikes.) The bikes, too, were the best racing models that money could buy, sadly lacking the baguette-wielding wicker basket up front that I thought came standard on any bicycle sold in Europe.

My favourite thing to do in Lucca was to sit on one of the *baluardos*, the arrow-shaped bulwarks that jut out at various points along the wall. I'd spend hours in the shade of the trees that grew there, my legs dangling over the walls, feasting on the crusty bread, cheeses and hams that I'd bought from a quaint *alimentari* just off the main square. From my vantage point I'd watch the world go by – a little less unobtrusively than the freaky old woman – or gaze across the jumbled terracotta roofs of the old city.

Lucca was mustard yellow. It had become apparent on my travels that Italian towns and cities were always one predominant colour. Castell'Arquato, with its medieval buildings hewn from rock, had a golden sandstone-coloured glow. Vernazza was pink. And now Lucca was a washed-out mustard yellow, complemented rather fetchingly by battered red terracotta tiles, weathered and faded by time and the elements.

The thing that struck me most over the few days I stayed in Lucca, however, was how stylish it was. Via Fillungo, Lucca's main shopping thoroughfare, was barely wide enough for two bicycles to pass each other. It featured Art Nouveau shop fronts and was home to all of Italy's best-known designers and a few I hadn't heard of as well. I'd peer in at the clothes, amazed by how gaudy, yet somehow still very, very cool, they were. Despite my *La Dolce Vita* fantasies, I knew I would never be able to carry off such clothes, even though I was the owner of a very spiffy Vespa. The good Lord has blessed me with a broad chest and a low centre of gravity, rather than the long, lean rock-star figure needed to wear these outfits and not look ridiculous. Still, I was drawn to them, particularly a pair of battered jeans with a fly you laced up with a leather cord. They were the sort of thing Michael Hutchence would have worn, and totally impractical of course, but I was inexplicably attracted to them.

It wasn't just the fashions that screamed out style. A small restaurant on one of the city's tiny lanes hung red glasses with candles in them from a nearby window grate at night for an effect that was both cultured and intimate. The Torre del Guinigi, a fifteenth-century tower, has an oak tree growing on top – I mean, how stylish is that? And in a manner befitting the city that gave us the composer Giaccomo Puccini and continued to inspire him as he wrote some of the world's favourite operas, it was not unusual to hear singers and musicians practising and polishing their work as you strolled past their stunning homes. In Lucca it seemed like everyone was pursuing some higher endeavour. I began to feel conspicuous.

Lucca was so stylish that it even elevated an event like a sweaty rock concert to sophisticated levels. Each July the city holds a Summer Festival, a series of concerts in Piazza Napoleone. The square was named after Napoleon by his sister, Elisa Baciocchi, who ruled Lucca from 1805 to 1815, and it would have to be one of the most beautiful settings for a concert around. The festival was due to start when I arrived and the programme boasted artists like Paul Simon, David Bowie, Oasis, Rod Stewart and Jamiroquai.

As settings for a rock concert go, Piazza Napoleone was unique. The stage was set up in front of the Palazzo Ducale, an impressive building knocked up in the Mannerist style by Ammannati in 1578 and once home to Lucca's rulers. Concertgoers could mingle among the oak trees, chill out on stone benches or, if they were lucky enough to be staying in the Hotel Universo, watch the show from their balcony. But what impressed me most when I went to see Jamiroquai were the Portaloos. They were set up in a line at one end of the square, each cloaked by a potted Cyprus pine brought in especially for the occasion. Well, that and the fact that the businesses around the square continued to operate during the performances and I could buy a gelato in the middle of 'Love Foolosophy'.

I think I must have had too much time on my hands in Lucca because I decided to do something about my appearance. Nothing too rash, like buying a pair of Michael Hutchence jeans. Rather, I thought I'd start with something simple like a haircut. The local folk all looked stylish and well groomed.

Perhaps if I used the same hairdresser I could too.

Experience has taught me that getting your hair cut overseas is not a good idea. A friend who decided on a haircut in the Maldives was alarmed when the barber placed a bowl on his head and cut around it. (The look was compounded when he lost his glasses and had to buy a new pair in Sri Lanka.) But I figured this was Italy, a global centre of style. What could go wrong?

Fate tried her hardest to intervene. When I went to have my hair cut the hairdresser's was closed. It was a Monday, you see. And Mondays are a designated day off for hairdressers. Not content with a huge siesta in the middle of each day, Italian workers also get one day off from their particular trades each week. Hairdressers on Mondays. Greengrocers on Wednesday afternoons. And so on, depending on what day their union has negotiated for them. I tell you, I wish I worked in Italy.

I returned the next morning and was ushered to a far corner of the salon where a flouncing hairdresser examined my hair with the same disdain he would a dead rat. He picked at it indiscriminately, holding various parts with his fingertips as if he was going to catch something. Then he called for an assistant, a young girl with a collection of interesting piercings, who handed him a battery of implements as if she was a nurse in *ER*. The hairdresser attacked my hair vigorously and seemingly without purpose. After thirty minutes he presented the finished effort with a dismissive wave.

It was the worst haircut I had ever had. My hairline is receding yet he had somehow fashioned what was left into a long fringe that swept across my forehead and covered my left eyebrow. I noted with alarm that it didn't look so different from the hairstyle sported by the female smurf I got in my Kinder Surprise that morning. The guy must have seen the look of horror on my face, because he stormed off in a huff. He spoke angrily with one of the girls in the salon who could speak English and after a while she came over to me.

'He says it was the best he could do with your hair,' she said. 'It was full of trouble.'

I christened the haircut a Lucca Fringe and used the reflection in the first shop window I saw to 'adjust' it into something less startling. If I forced a centre part it didn't look so bad, the only discordant note being an unusually long wisp of hair that tickled my right ear. I had hoped to step out of the hairdresser's looking a little more like Marcello Mastroianni. Instead I bore an uncanny resemblance to the keyboard player in Flock of Seagulls.

Any sensible person would have learned from their mistake but I compounded the problem by buying a pair of slip-on sandals. I'd only brought shoes with me to Italy – to protect my feet, as I'd been taught at the motorcycle course back in Sydney. But the heat of early summer meant that my feet were being stewed instead.

And it wasn't as if my feet needed protecting, anyway. On a normal motorbike they would be exposed to all kinds of dangers. But the ingenious design of the Vespa means that the front aprons protect the rider's legs from dust and rain and the cowls covering the engine keep oil and grease at bay. An old issue of *Motociclismo Magazine* I have come across since claims it is another reason why Vespas have proven to be so popular with women and even businessmen. The Vespa, it said, is the 'ideal vehicle for short town trips for businessmen, men of the professions and doctors, who may park it in a public parking place and present themselves for their appointments looking as perfect as though they had just got out of a car'. It also meant that I could wear the minimum of footwear.

The sandals I ended up buying looked cool in the window. They even looked okay when I tried them on in the shop, assisted by a guy with a haircut that looked suspiciously like a Lucca Fringe. But in the harsh light of the mid-afternoon sun and combined with my hastily altered Lucca Fringe, the sandals looked very camp. Worse, I knew in my heart that Marcello Mastroianni would *never* have been seen dead in them.

I decided to stay in Lucca until Sally arrived. It was only 15 kilometres from Pisa, 40 from Livorno. The gelato was good and the spectacular Garfagnana Mountains virtually backed on to the city. It was the perfect base for exploring north-western Tuscany.

The hostel had worked out well, too. It was clean and cheap and the situation in my dorm was more bearable now that Old Farty Pants had left to terrorise another hostel somewhere else in Italy. He'd been replaced by two middle-aged guys from Perth with matching moustaches. One of them had owned a Vespa in Perth in the 1960s and whenever I came back to the dorm – either after a day out or simply from having a shower – he'd warn me of things that, by bitter experience, he knew could go wrong with old Vespas.

'Always give the spark plug a scrub,' he said one night. Another time he gave me a dire warning about rust in the tank. He had obviously suffered and was determined I wouldn't have to.

After I'd seen pretty much everything Lucca had to offer, I began making short excursions into the countryside around the town. It was a beautiful area of green hills dotted with stately villas. I'd start each morning at the café attached to the railway station. I liked the buzz of the place, and I would linger at the solid marble bar, sipping my cappuccino and nibbling my doughnut, longer than I should have. Commuters on their way to Pisa or Livorno or some big city in the region would stride in purposefully, ordering their coffee, knocking back espresso like it was a shot and then slamming their cups down. It struck me that this was probably the most active, the most focused, they'd be all day. It would be siesta time by 12.30 and, I don't care what Italians say, I can't believe anyone is particularly productive after a three-hour lunch break.

Next I would call into the Shell petrol station for some fuel. Gianni had told me to pull into a Shell service station whenever I saw the sign for one. 'More octane!' he'd said. He reckoned that the extra octane in Shell Ultra would make Sophia's old engine work better. I'd done as he said and, to be honest, hadn't noticed any difference from when I used Agip or Fina. But Gianni wasn't the only one convinced of the special qualities of Shell Ultra. Even Roberto, the rough-hewn farmer who had given me a chunk of ham in Broni, had made the same suggestion. I suspect that it was because Shell sponsored the Ferrari Formula One team. The Italians are crazy for Formula One and think Michael Schumacher is a saint. The fact that the petrol attendant at the Shell station in Lucca had a signed photo of Michael Schumacher on his desk only confirmed my theory.

Having both refuelled, Sophia and I would set off on one of our excursions. Nothing too adventurous, just something to fill in a lazy morning or afternoon. One day it was a trip to Ponte della Maddalena, a hump-backed stone bridge that spanned the River Serchio just north of Borgo a Mozzano. It is also known as the Devil's Bridge, after a local tale that claims it was built for the village by the devil in return for the possession of the first soul to cross it. Legend has it that the villagers agreed and, when it was finished, sent a dog across.

Another day I visited Collodi, a small town famous for its Baroque villa and a theme park dedicated to Pinocchio. The guy who wrote the original story of Pinocchio back in the 1880s was a Florentine journalist called Carlo Lorenzini. He released the book using the pen name Carlo Collodi, after the town – apparently he'd holidayed there as a child – and the town repaid the favour by building a theme park to celebrate his creation.

The Italian version of Pinocchio is somewhat darker than Disney's. In it Pinocchio is just as likely to squash Jiminy Cricket against a wall as listen to one of his annoying songs. I guess that's why the Pinocchio of Parco di Pinocchio looks more like a freaky android from *Terminator II* than the cuddly cartoon creation. It has heavily jointed legs and demonic eyes and peers out threateningly from every corner of the park, which I have to say is one of the crappiest theme parks I've ever had the misfortune of shelling out €7 for. There was an outdoor theatre that didn't show anything and a really sad maze – a *labirinto*, as the Italians like to call it – made from thin bamboo screens. The worst part was the diorama that told the story of Pinocchio using tatty papier-mâché figures. It was accompanied by a recording of a cat going 'Miaow! Miaow! Miaow!' and cost an extra euro to get in.

Back in town there was an overabundance of souvenir shops selling all kinds of Pinocchio-related junk – pencils, plates, placemats, T-shirts, teatowels, snowdomes and cups. And that's not to mention Pinocchios of all sizes, from tiny wooden dolls on a string to freestanding ones the size of a small child. One stall owner, particularly bored, pointed out a particularly monstrous one and said, 'Fine craftsmanship!'

Impressed that he could even be bothered to make that much effort I struck up a conversation with him. Business was slow. More and more Italian households had VCRs, and Italian kids were now more familiar with Disney's Pinocchio than the authentic Italian one.

'Only the tourists they buy them,' he complained. 'The kids say, "That'sa not Pinocchio. He looksa different on da video!"'

On the way back to Lucca from Collodi I stopped at an intersection, and because Sophia was old and under-powered I waited a bit longer for the traffic to pass than most Italians were used to. Well, more than the guy in the Alfa behind me was used to. He ran up the back of me. The collision was slight – not enough to cause any major damage – but I heard a strange 'pop' from the front of the bike. I was put off checking it out any further by the ferocity of the guy's wife gesticulating at me.

When I arrived back at the hostel I told one of the Perth moustache men what had happened and he came down and looked at my Vespa. There was a star-shaped explosion of black oil around the centre of the front wheel, a result, it would seem, of the popping noise I had heard.

'Looks like a wheel bearing shit itself,' he said stroking his moustache. 'Never happened to me, though, so I wouldn't put money on it.'

We both stood back looking at Sophia, in the way blokes do, as if looking hard enough or long enough would reveal more about the problem or even mysteriously repair it. I knew there was only person I could ask who would know for sure. The Waspmaster.

It was time to give him a call.

CHAPTER EIGHT

Livorno

Kinder Surprise Toy: Teapot Warrior
(K02-048)

It was The Waspmaster who had originally pointed out to me that there was a 1961 Vespa for sale on eBay. Over the five days I was bidding for Sophia The Waspmaster and I had been in regular email correspondence. It wasn't until the third email between us that I discovered that his real name was Filippo and that he ran a Vespa import–export business in Livorno.

When the auction finally finished and I emerged victorious, Filippo was the first to email his congratulations. I emailed him back to tell him I owed him a beer when I got to Livorno. Now I was to meet him face-to-face.

Livorno is only 40 kilometres south of Lucca but I set off early in the morning while the air was still crisp. I took a route that skirted Pisa, cutting through farmland before joining the S1, a minor road lined by tall pines. It ran beside Camp Darby, a huge American army base that went on for kilometres, surrounded by chainwire fencing and dotted with watchtowers manned by thick-necked marines.

Livorno came into view soon after the army camp ended, and if I hadn't had business to attend to there I would have kept going. It is Italy's second biggest port and its skyline bristled with cranes and smokestacks. The approach to the city was grimy and polluted and lined with container depots and compounds engaged in the business of importing and exporting. The road was a nightmare, pot-holed and broken by the stream of semi-trailers that trundled along it relentlessly. Sophia bounced along it like a bronco in a rodeo.

I had arranged to meet Filippo outside the Hotel Gran Duca, down near the harbour. When I arrived he was already there, waiting in his Citroën Méhari beside the brass statue of Duke Ferdinand I. Filippo was in his late twenties and with his shaved head, goatee beard and psuedo-Limp Bizkit wardrobe he could have passed for an American college student. But there was something about his grooming and the way he sauntered in his three-quarter-length cargo shorts that could only be Italian.

Filippo's Méhari gave off the same vibes. It was like an oversized Mini Moke, and with its lack of doors and makeshift canvas roof you could almost imagine it cruising the beaches of California. But it was French, and the particularly Gallic touches, like the bizarre pressed panelling, meant it would only seem right in places like this – by the sea in Italy and France – and probably nowhere else.

I followed Filippo along the waterfront to Viale Italia, a road that hugs the shoreline, towards a Vespa museum and workshop run by his business partner, Marco. Livorno was more alluring here. An attempt had been made to landscape the rocky waterfront with walkways and grassy squares, and it is lined by impressive stands of palm trees that give the place a slight French Riviera feel. Girls wearing little more than a bikini, a sarong and a cool pair of sunglasses buzzed by us on motor scooters on their way to the beach, adding to the Riviera ambience.

Marco's workshop was in a basement beneath an apartment building only a block away from the beach. Whereas Filippo was pure Fred Durst, Marco looked like a character out of *La Dolce Vita* – a mop of curly hair, sideburns and cool 1960s-style glasses. He was immaculately dressed in cords and a collared shirt. That he restored Vespas dressed like this, still in his Campers, said he was more of an artist than a mechanic.

Marco was working on a 1972 Super Sport and

motioned for me to have a look around his workshop while he finished adjusting the clutch cable. Filippo showed me all the different Vespas Marco was restoring and pointed out a display cabinet with model Vespas and toys from all over the world.

'People send them to Marco as a way of saying thanks,' he explained. 'He's got stuff from Germany, Spain, England, even the USA.'

The walls of the workshop were lined with promotional posters and calendars that Piaggio had produced over the decades. They included a famous 1954 calendar drawn by Franco Mosca featuring illustrations of 'sophisticated' women lounging on Vespas. These calendars were an innovation pioneered by Piaggio and the portraits of attractive girls doing exciting things like skiing, picnicking and travelling helped give Vespas an aura of cheeky likeability. The calendars pre-dated the more famous Pirelli ones – in fact, Pirelli are the first to admit they pinched the idea from Vespa. But unlike the Pirelli girls, the Vespa girls, as they became known, were more than just pin-ups. They were portrayed as air hostesses, international travellers and Oxford scholars – feisty, independent women, in other words.

I spotted the Vespa calendar for 1962, the year I was born, just to the left of the pinball machine.

'That was the first year they used actresses as models in the calendars,' said Filippo. 'It was so popular they did it again the next year. Piaggio got 10,000 letters from Indonesia alone!'

Apart from the fabulous Vespa memorabilia, what struck me immediately about the workshop was how spotless it was. You could run your finger along any surface, even the floor under the bikes Marco was working on, and the only grime on it would be your body's natural oils.

Marco's workshop was obviously a kind of drop-in centre for people who wanted advice, parts, a chat or to simply watch him work. It was something he encouraged by keeping an old round-edged fridge full of beer, Coca-Cola and *acqua minerale*. There was a couch for people to sit on as they watched Marco work, and a stereo and a pinball machine for when they got bored.

That afternoon a girl called Ajeuna dropped by. She breezed in, chatted for a little while, then turned her attention to a quick game of pinball, which she played sucking on a beer she had grabbed from the fridge. Then without warning, and midway through the game, she put the beer down, kissed Marco and then left with a big 'Ciao!'

'She is full of *brio*!' Marco said with a smile.

Marco was soon finished with the cable on the Super Sport and told me to bring in Sophia so he could have a closer look at her. I felt like a nervous exhibitor at an antiques fair. The first thing he did was confirm that she was a 1961 model. I asked him how he knew.

'The choke under the seat,' he pointed out. 'And the colour. By 1962 it was a light blue.'

He pulled off the cowl and looked for the VN number. To an untrained eye, like mine, it looked like an unrelated batch of ten numbers. But to someone like Marco it read like a potted history, telling him the exact model, the year it was made and even which factory it was made in. It confirmed his 1961 theory.

'The tail light is not authentic,' he said. 'And the original did not have a mirror.'

He circled Sophia a couple of more times and then passed his judgment.

'It is a good solid example of the marque,' he said. 'You got it for a good price.' I felt chuffed. It meant a lot coming from an expert like Marco.

I pointed out the splotch of oil on the front wheel and Marco declared that the front shock absorber had blown.

'I have one here,' he said. 'I can fix it now if you like.'

Marco didn't wear overalls when he worked. He simply plucked a pair of surgical gloves from a nearby dispenser and snapped them onto his hands like a doctor about to do an anal probe. He wheeled Sophia onto a small purpose-built stand and quickly removed the old shock absorber and replaced it with a new one. He called out the name of tools as he needed them and Filippo grabbed them off the wall, where they were all methodically hung, each in its own special place, and handed them to him. I noticed that there was a corkscrew among the spanners. I liked the way this guy worked.

While Marco had Sophia on the stand he checked the electrical system and decided to change the coil and the condenser as well. They were old and worn and only emitted a rather sad orange spark to the spark plug. Once they were replaced a big blue spark leapt from beneath the spark plug cap to the spark plug, even if you held them a couple of centimetres apart.

'A tempest of electricity!' Marco announced proudly as he put the appropriate covers back on.

Marco concluded Sophia's check-up by putting a sticker on the petrol cap saying how much oil should go in and fitting bone-coloured rubber protectors on the clutch and brake handles. I stood back and admired Sophia as she ticked over contentedly on the stand. It was like she was a new bike.

I asked Marco how much I owed him for the work and after conferring with Filippo in Italian he waved his hands in an expansive manner.

'We have a figure in mind,' he said finally. 'But we'd prefer to take you to dinner. You can buy the wine.'

I left Sophia in Marco's workshop and the three of us piled into Filippo's Méhari. As we left the workshop I had pointed to Marco's display of Vespa toys and told him about my quest for the Kinder Surprise Vespa (I'd got a rather silly kitchen pot soldier only that morning).

Marco was intrigued. 'Kinder Surprise?' he asked. 'If you find an extra one I would like it for my collection.'

As we drove back towards the centre of town Filippo gave a running commentary on the history of Livorno. He had lived in London during his teens – his dad had been the trade ambassador to Britain – so his English was perfect.

'Livorno was a swamp,' he shouted over the road noise kicked up by the Méhari. 'But when Pisa's harbour silted up they decided to build the new harbour here. It was populated by criminals, hookers and scum. That's why we Livornese are so lively!'

To prove his point, Filippo drove right up close to a Mercedes with Pisa numberplates that was dawdling along the sea front. It was occupied by an old couple who were looking at the view.

'Too slow,' he shouted after them as we wove around them in the Méhari.

The so-called 'criminals, hookers and scum' of whom Filippo spoke so fondly were the Jews, Protestants, Arabs and Turks who flocked to the town when it was declared a free port in 1608, open to all traders regardless of religion, race or, indeed, shady past. It quickly became Italy's most 'colourful' port and, as a consequence, its most successful.

That the Livornese are still keen to live life to the fullest was evident near the sea front, where the streets were packed solid with parked scooters. The girls were out again, but this time they were better dressed and were doubling their girlfriends, who all seemed to be busily chatting on mobile phones. It struck me that this was a modern version of the Italian movies I had watched as a teenager. A version where the girls, dressed in designer sunnies and clutching the latest mobile phones, turned up at nightclubs and bars on Vespas while the blokes waited for them to arrive.

Vespas have been a liberating force for women in Italy. Because they were reliable and easy to ride the tiny wasps represented independence for the post-war generation. Piaggio were aware of this. The first pamphlet produced to promote the Vespa made a point of showing a woman driver (the radical step-through frame was inspired by a woman's bicycle). Riding a Vespa was a breeze and it was fun. Even the calendars, which were designed primarily to titillate, portrayed women in exotic settings doing adventurous and exciting things. So, while it wasn't exactly Germaine Greer, the Vespa was liberating in its own way.

We began our night out in Livorno with an *aperitivo* at a wine bar, one of three on a tiny lane where the footpath was littered with Vespas. Filippo said all Italians loved their pre-meal *aperitivo*. 'It opens your stomach,' he said. But when he set off to check which wine bar we should go to – the classic one, the trendy one or the normal one – Marco told me there was more to the *aperitivo* than any dubious gastronomic effect it may have. It was more about *farsi vedere* – being seen.

'The right wine bar to be seen in is always changing,' explained Marco. 'That is why Filippo is checking to see which one it is tonight.'

A few minutes later Filippo returned and ushered us towards the traditional wine bar. It seemed I was about to enter an inner sanctum of that Italian cool I had first seen flickering on a black and white television all those years ago as a teenager. But Italian cool is an ephemeral thing, and even as we sat down Filippo was on his mobile phone to other friends, checking whether the goalposts had moved and if the real action was happening elsewhere.

I was more than happy with the traditional wine bar. With its mirrored walls and subtle lighting it was the kind of place you'd expect Marcello Mastroianni to saunter into with an elegant woman on his arm. The barman wore an immaculately tailored black suit and a crisp white shirt, and upon opening a bottle of wine for us he deftly swished any cork that may have crumbled into a stainless-steel sink. A complimentary plate of boar's liver bruschetta graced the bar. Quite a change from the packet of crisps I was used to back home.

After an hour of seeing and being seen, we clambered back into the Méhari and raced off down a series of dark and dingy roads to Al Giro Di Boa, a restaurant hidden among the back streets of Livorno. It looked like a very bad student restaurant back home, right down to an amateurish painting of King Neptune on the back wall to indicate that yes, it served seafood. We were taken past the kitchen and out the back to a concrete yard full of plastic tables and tatty umbrellas that had been given to the restaurant by Campari maybe a decade or two before.

Filippo must have noticed my surprise because he felt compelled to comment. 'It doesn't look much, but the food is fantastic,' he said enthusiastically.

A bored waitress eventually emerged from inside and Filippo ordered a selection of local specialties. We started with anchovies – large fillets laid out in a daisy pattern – and then followed it with *riso negro*, a rice dish made black from squid's ink, and smoked swordfish. Filippo was right. It *was* fantastic. And the two bottles of Italian white I'd picked up back at the wine bar – as payment for services rendered – went down exceedingly easily as well.

The conversation turned to my plans and I told them how I hoped to export Sophia back to Australia when I had finished my journey in Italy.

Filippo warned me I could have problems. He and Marco sometimes sent bikes to the US and only the other day a customs official had confronted him about exporting Italian heritage. 'I told him I was saving it from the government,' he said. 'Thanks to their *rotamazione* programme there are hardly any old bikes left.'

Rotamazione was a policy introduced by the

government to try and meet EU emission controls. A variation of the Italian word for rotation, it was an attempt to get old scooters off the road and encourage people to buy new ones. The owners of old scooters receive €1000 when they trade them in. The downside is that the scooters then have to be scrapped.

'They can be used for spares,' interrupted Marco. 'But as spares they're only worth a few hundred euros. Why sell them for that when the government will give you €1000 towards a new bike?'

I asked Filippo why they didn't buy the old Vespas from the dealers before they were scrapped.

'It is very strictly controlled,' he said. 'Even in Italy there is no way around this law.'

Marco and Filippo saw the *rotamazione* policy as a conspiracy between the Italian government and Piaggio to sell more scooters. But the reality was that the government was bowing to pressure from the EU. According to the environmental group the Bluewater Network, a week of commuting on a 40-horsepower, two-stroke scooter is the hydrocarbon equivalent of driving 100,000 miles in a car. Put simply, the time for dirty old two-stroke engines has passed.

We finished the meal with a *ponce*, a Livornese drink made of rum, coffee and sugar and finished with a piece of lemon peel. *Ponce* is a mispronunciation of the English word 'punch', and was an attempt by the Livornese to make the royal navy rum brought into the port by English sailors more palatable. Marco was quite a connoisseur of the stuff. He explained that the rum was from the Antilles and because it was rough and strong the Livornese added coffee and sugar. A *ponce* with a small piece of lemon skin floating in it, like the ones we were drinking, were called *ponce a vela*.

'*A vela* means with a sailor,' he explained. 'The Livornese used to think the skin of the lemon looked like the skin of a sailor.'

After I downed my *ponce* and declared it a mighty fine drink, it was decided that we should visit Bar Civili, an institution that Marco grandly claimed was the 'most famous *ponce* bar in the world'. It was back near the railway station, hidden among blocks of faded and worn apartments, so we settled the bill, clambered back into the Méhari and set off again into the Livornese night.

The Civili has been open for over 100 years, a self-proclaimed 'bar, meeting place, institution and temple to continuity'. It was small and cosy, with arches and wooden beams that appeared lower than they were because of all the football pennants stuck to them. The walls were covered with evocative black and white photographs of old Livorno and paintings that were presented to the bar to settle the huge *ponce* tabs the artists had run up. The most famous, an impressionistic representation of Livorno's harbour at sunset, was by Renato Natali, one of Italy's most famous post-Macchiaioli artists.

The bar attracted a mixed crowd. Cool girls with bindis sipped on Persiana, a startling green drink named after the colour of Livorno's window shutters, while old guys in cloth caps sat at tables drinking beer and soda, another particularly Livornese beverage. Elsewhere a group of thirty-something men were playing cards. At the bar, a salty old sea captain, looking like something out of a Robert Louis Stevenson novel, was knocking back *ponce* like he was about to go to sea for a decade or two. With a wave of his hand Marco ordered three more *ponce* and we joined the old sea dog at the bar. We had barely finished our first drinks when Filippo decided that a tour of the canals was in order.

Livorno's canals are in Piccola Venezia, an area originally laid out in the late sixteenth century using land reclamation methods tried and tested by the Venetians on the other side of the country. While the comparisons with Venice are a little fanciful, the stately apartments that line them, complete with shutters painted persiana green, give the canals a certain charm, as do the remains of the old fort built in 1590 that backs onto them on the other side.

Filippo had the keys to one of the grotto boatsheds that lines the narrowest of the canals and instructed Marco and me to grab a fuel tank and take it down to the nearby wharf. He wheeled out a trolley with a small outboard engine on it and followed us.

Down at the wharf Filippo chose a small boat,

seemingly at random, and attached the engine to the back of it. We clambered aboard and Filippo started the engine.

Standing as he held the throttle bar, he looked a little demented. 'Time for the *tarpone* trip!' he declared tipsily.

Tarpones are rats that live near the canals in Livorno. 'As big as cats!' according to Filippo. The noise of the boat would startle them into diving into the canals to swim away from the perceived threat. Within seconds I had spotted my first.

We puttered around the canals aimlessly, chugging under low bridges and turning onto other canals on a whim. It was past midnight now so the waterways were largely deserted. The only other vessel we saw was a fishing boat returning with the night's catch. We motored peacefully through stone tunnels, centuries old, and alongside the high brick walls of the fort. The Communist Party was holding a fundraising event here, under the palm trees, and drunken revellers waved to us as we passed. My favourite part, and a place popular with the *tarpone*, was the waterside entrance to Livorno's huge market. A cobbled path led down to the water, secured by a grilled gate not dissimilar to the type musketeers are always foiled by when escaping from dungeons in old movies.

Marco and I sat at the front of the boat with our feet up and hands behind our heads, content to soak up the atmosphere of the canals at night. As we chug-a-lugged back to the dock and the boatshed, a cool breeze mopped our brows and tickled our ears. I was experiencing a side of Italy I would never have seen if I hadn't met Marco and Filippo. And let's face it, I would never have met them if I hadn't bought an old Vespa on the Internet. Thanks to Sophia I'd just had one of the most sublime evenings of my life.

The smell of the sea air seemed to invigorate Filippo and by the time we had lugged the motor and the fuel tank back he had gotten his second wind. 'Let's go to Station Galleri!' he cried, and before I could catch my breath we were back in the Méhari and hurtling towards Castiglioncello, along a road lined with oleander that hugged the coast. 'This road was built by the Romans,' said Filippo as he threw the car around treacherous bends. 'The marble from Carrara came this way.'

Closer to Castiglioncello Marco pointed out a house built on a cliff overlooking the sea that Marcello Mastroianni had once lived in. The road down to Castiglioncello struck me as the kind of road Marcello would drive along in one of his movies – late at night, in a convertible Fiat or Alfa, with a large-breasted woman wearing a head scarf beside him. In the movies, the sea would remain unseen, as it was now, but its brooding presence – which, as a teenager I considered a metaphor for sex – could always be felt.

Station Galleri, it turns out, was a bar run by a

flamboyant chap who seemed particularly happy to see Filippo.

'You will see all kinds of people here,' said Filippo, ignoring the owner's obvious interest. 'The barman lets everyone in.'

We were shown to a small table at the back, away from the few other people in the place who sat slumped in their chairs, their heads on the table, and the remains of that one drink too far beside them. Filippo immediately texted one of his girlfriends, an Armenian girl who worked as an exotic dancer, to see what time she got off.

I told him that I had never texted anyone before I met Sally, but I was hooked. It was fun. It was romantic.

Filippo agreed and said that he believed texting had revolutionised flirting. 'It leaves things unsaid,' he said with a smile.

Then Filippo spotted a friend, Daniella. She was an elegant brunette who looked like a 1960s model, the sort you'd see lounging on a Vespa in a Piaggio calendar shoot. She had incredibly long legs that she tucked up underneath herself and sat dragging on a cigarette languorously. They retired to a cushion room at the back to talk, drink peach schnapps and cognac, and flirt.

Marco ordered another *ponce* – surprise, surprise – and I asked him if he was kept busy restoring bikes. He nodded and said that a collector from Milan was sending him two or three bikes a month to restore.

The man had twenty-seven in all, ranging from a 1946 Vespa 98 to one of the first Primaveras, and as Marco finished restoring one lot the guy would send more.

I can understand why a collector would want Marco to restore his bikes. The bikes Marco restored were beyond brand new – they had a glow, almost an aura, about them. Marco admitted with a shy grin that he signed inside the cowl of each bike he restored.

'My Vespas are like my children,' he said. 'I am like a mother and her child. When I restore one I don't like to let them go into the world.'

After the bar closed at 4 am we drove back along the coast road to Livorno. I was too tipsy to ride Sophia back to Lucca now and, besides, the hostel locked its doors at midnight. Marco said I could sleep on the floor of the workshop, so I pulled the cushions off the sofa and laid them out under the watchful eye of Giovanna Ralli, Miss July 1962, who was wearing a chocolate-brown bikini and flower-encrusted swimming cap as she sipped a Campari.

There was a strong smell of two-stroke. I drifted off to sleep and had a nagging dream that I couldn't find Sophia. In fact she was sitting on a ramp in the workshop beside me.

CHAPTER NINE

Pontedera

Kinder Surprise Toy: Robotic Toolman
(K02-042)

I woke the next morning to find Marco and Filippo shaking me gently and peering into my face. They appeared to be no worse for wear from the night before – indeed, Marco was immaculately groomed as always. But they seemed very concerned about my wellbeing. They were right to be so. I had consumed a variety of alcoholic beverages, most of which I had never heard of before and which contained generous portions of rum. I hadn't showered since I left the hostel in Lucca. And I'd slept in the clothes I'd been wearing. But really, apart from the slight taste of gasoline at the back of my throat, I didn't feel that bad.

Marco had to pick up some parts from the Vespa factory in Pontedera and asked me if I wanted to tag along. It was only 20 kilometres away and in a round-about fashion it was on the way back to Lucca, where my worldly possessions were sitting beside a bunk bed I'd paid for but hadn't used. Filippo said there was a museum in the factory there that I might find interesting.

When the Piaggio factory opened in Pontedera in 1924 it made aeroplane engines, at first under licence from companies in France and Britain, but later from designs produced by its own engineers. It was one of many expansions into heavy industry in the early part of the twentieth century by Piaggio. First established in 1887, Piaggio was already building ships in Sestri Ponente in the Liguria region (they were renowned for their extravagant Art Nouveau interiors) and railway rolling stock in Finale Ligure. When all the big Italian industrial companies like Fiat, Breda and Ansaldo had a sudden desire to take to the air it was only natural that Piaggio would follow suit. By building a new aero-nautical factory in the Arno Valley, Piaggio were in effect protecting their interests.

Not surprisingly, the fact they were building planes made the Piaggio factory at Pontedera a prime target of Allied bombing raids during World War II. By January 1944 the workshops were almost totally destroyed and any machinery that hadn't been requisitioned by the Germans and shipped back to Berlin was moved to Biella, in Piedmont, in the far north-west of the country. At the end of the war the wide open space around what was left of the factory was used by the occupying American army as a makeshift camp. Not long after the site was back under Piaggio's control and the few men and machinery that remained were put to work making aluminium pots and pans.

Enrico Piaggio, the ambitious chairman who had overseen the company's massive expansion between the wars, knew that he would not be able to rebuild the company by making frypans. He set his best engineers the task of developing a product around which the company could rebuild. Something for a country still on its knees and strewn with rubble. A few months later, his most brilliant aeronautical engineer, Corradino D'Ascanio, presented him with drawings of a prototype motor scooter. Piaggio laconically commented that the pinched waistline and rounded sides made it look like a *vespa*, a wasp. But he still had the foresight to order the production of 10,000 of them. On 23 April 1946 an application was lodged in the patent office in Florence. By 1953 the 500,000th Vespa rolled off the production line – blessed by the Archbishop of Pisa, no less – and the factory was employing over 3800 people.

I followed Filippo's Méhari on Sophia. It was nice to have a breeze on my face and Filippo chose to take a more circuitous route to Pontedera that followed a canal through fields of blooming sunflowers. We were only kilometres from the Arno Valley, one of the country's largest industrial conurbations, yet we were trundling through countryside that looked like something out of a Frances Mayes desktop calendar.

The Piaggio factory, however, was ugly. The façade of the entrance had the odd Art Deco flourish – it was one of the few parts of the factory to escape the bombing – but elsewhere it looked like any industrial site thrown up in the late 1940s, and had seen little maintenance since.

As motor museums go it wasn't too bad. The entrance hall was lined with an archive stuffed with historical documents and promotional material, and the main hall housed examples of nearly every type of vehicle that Piaggio had ever made. There were scooters, planes, cars and even a tiny *Ape* fire engine, and in typical Italian fashion everything was presented with a certain style and panache.

Marco and Filippo were regular visitors and each had their favourite displays. Filippo liked the Paratrooper Vespa, with its army-green paint job and grenade launcher. Marco had a soft spot for the prototypes, the ugly first attempts at creating a Vespa, which came with bicycle pumps to inflate the tyres. They visited these models first and then reverentially walked around the displays as if they were in church, stopping at different Vespas, stroking their chins and pondering each exhibit, as if it would reveal the meaning of life.

His soul suitably soothed, Marco wandered off to find the parts he needed. Filippo came over to join me in front of what was in fact a huge 'bookshelf', three Vespas high and six across, and asked me what I thought. I told him I was impressed that they found someone to build a display cabinet that fitted so many bikes.

'Marco won't tell you himself but he restored a lot of these bikes,' he said, pointing at the bikeshelf. 'Including that 1961 model just like yours.'

When Marco returned I asked him whether what Filippo told me was true.

He nodded his head sheepishly. 'It had never been ridden,' he said, 'But it was damaged in the 1966 floods. Getting the mud out was the hardest part.'

When the River Arno burst its banks and flooded the Uffizi in 1966, countless pieces of priceless artwork were destroyed or damaged. In Pontedera it was the River Era that burst its banks. A wall of water and mud poured into the factory buildings, extinguishing the smelting moulds, covering machinery and ruining half-finished and finished Vespas on the production line. Umberto Agnelli, who had become president of the company on the death of his father-in-law, Enrico Piaggio, said it was like looking at 'a modern-day Pompeii'. Cases containing plastic components and other lightweight materials were found halfway along the road between Pontedera and Pisa.

'The workers all came in and helped to clean up,'

said Filippo. 'The production line was up and running again in four days!'

When we walked back out of the museum we found a young guy with a backpack admiring Sophia, which was parked in the courtyard. He was a New Zealander and a self-proclaimed Vespa nut, and had taken a moment out of his hectic Eurail itinerary to visit the Vespa factory. He was very taken with my Vespa and asked if I would photograph him standing next to her.

'She's so beautiful, man!' he said excitedly, as I handed his camera back. 'The accessories are awesome!'

I spotted Marco and Filippo smirking. 'You'd better be careful,' said Filippo. 'She'll run off with someone who treats her better.'

The Piaggio factory is something of a Mecca for Vespa owners. They come from all over the world to visit – indeed many of the European Vespa clubs make an annual pilgrimage specially to pay homage. A pack of riders from the Hagan Vespa Club in Switzerland had gathered outside the museum that day and were performing impromptu repairs and modifications in a far corner of the carpark. They rode PXs primarily, the Vespa model brought out in 1977 and still manufactured today. But it seemed to me that their tinkering went against everything Corradino D'Ascanio had fought for when he designed the Vespa in the first place. He'd put the engine at the back of the bike and covered it so you didn't need to deal with it. He'd hated the oil and grease of conventional motorcycles. These guys were revelling in it.

Travelling by Vespa that way certainly didn't appeal to me. They looked grubby and oily and hot in their sensible all-weather gear. It wasn't the sweet life, it was the sweat life. They also had enough tools and spare parts to cater for any contingency, which to me defeated the purpose of riding a Vespa in the first place. It was meant to be a carefree experience where whatever happened, happened. Sure, I'd been caught out a couple of times – being stranded in Ponte dell'Olio perhaps the most obvious – but look what had happened there. I had seen a beautiful part of Italy I would have otherwise missed and enjoyed perhaps the best meal of my life.

Marco saw me watching them and shook his head. 'It just doesn't look like fun, does it?' he said.

He'd read my mind. It didn't look like fun at all. It was as far removed from my teenage fantasies about riding a Vespa in Italy as was physically possible. I couldn't for the life of me imagine a young Sophia Loren sauntering up to these guys and asking for a ride. She'd be worried she'd get oil all over her dress.

As we were leaving, Filippo asked me if I'd like to join him and Marco and a group of friends at a pine-nut festival that night. It was held each year near Marina di Pisa, in the fields around San Piero a Grado, one of the oldest churches in Italy. It supposedly celebrated the annual harvest of pine nuts, but according to Filippo it was really just an excuse to drink, eat and party.

'You can shower at Marco's workshop,' said Filippo, pre-empting my concerns about the state of my personal hygiene. 'And you can borrow one of my shirts.'

Sagre (feasting festivals) have been a staple of Italian life since Roman times and the most famous, the Saturnalia, was a week of drunken revelry that culminated in a human sacrifice. Even now, on the flimsiest of pretexts, Italians will celebrate a harvest or good fortune with a slap-up feed and a bouncy castle for the kids. Santena in Piemonte has an asparagus festival. Alba in the same province has a truffle festival. And for the past twenty-three years the good folk near Marina di Pisa have had the *Sagra del Pinolo*, the Feast of the Pine Nut.

We set off from Marco's workshop just as the sun was setting. Marco rode with Filippo in the Méhari and I followed on Sophia. We were joined by Francesco, a young local artist, who rode an old Lambretta Marco had restored for him. We headed north, through the port and over freeway flyovers until we hit the coast and its faded beach-side resorts.

I felt like I was part of a cool beatnik gang. I don't know if it was because of our vehicles or the faded beach houses. It could well have been the fact that both Filippo and Francesco had goatees. Whatever it was, Filippo was our Dobie Gillis and we were a bunch of buddies heading off to a really 'happening' beach party.

At Terrenia we turned away from the coast and skirted through the forests just to the north of the American army base. The first sign that we had arrived at the festival were the cars parked at awkward angles beside the road, in a manner that suggested there had been a nuclear holocaust and the drivers had instantly vaporised. Filippo parked the Méhari where he could and got Francesco and me to double him and Marco the rest of the way.

The place was buzzing. People stood in large groups chatting, while their kids ran between their legs. A huge, open-sided marquee had been set up at one end of the field and it was already full of people sitting at the benches eating. Behind the marquee was a phalanx of huge barbecues fuelled by pine cones and manned by an army of chefs in white T-shirts and aprons who threw steaks onto the hotplates a dozen at a time.

Another tent had been set up especially to take food orders, so we wandered over. We ordered by ticking boxes on a menu with a sozzled-looking cartoon pine nut at the top, and joined the queue to hand it in.

I ordered a bowl of *spaghetti alla pignola* and a bottle of soft drink and got change from €4.

Filippo went off to search for his friends, Roccia and Rossana, and found them already eating at a table inside the marquee. Roccia was built like a boulder (hence his nickname – *roccia* is the Italian word for rock). He was short and stocky and as round as he was tall. His head was shaved, he had a goatee, too, and he spoke English with a cockney accent. He ran a clothing shop in Pisa called 'Made in England' and organised Northern Soul dance parties. His girlfriend, Rossana, was positively petite beside him, and had a Mod haircut and a Vespa T-shirt with a red, white and blue target symbol over each breast.

Roccia saved seats for us so we sat at the table chatting while we waited for our food to arrive.

'Hey, Filippo, why didn't you ride your *cugi* Vespa?' Roccia teased.

I'd never heard of a *cugi* Vespa before. I had heard of Primaveras. Gran Sports. Even Cosas. But I'd never seen anything about a *cugi* Vespa.

Noticing my perplexed look, Filippo explained. 'A *cugi* Vespa is a tacky one,' he explained. 'Like a car with furry dice.'

The word came from *cugini di campagna*, 'your cousins who live in the country', and was used for anything that was in bad taste. Filippo had accessorised his Vespa to be as tacky as possible. A white vinyl seat with a fringe. Green handles with coloured plastic streamers hanging off the handlebars, like dragster bicycles used to have when I was younger, and yellow trim and more chrome than Liberace's bathroom. He had even developed the Vespa version of a *doof-doof* sound system, selling off the glove box and setting the speakers in its place for that extra heavy bass sound.

I told him that it sounded truly awful.

'It is!' he laughed. 'But it is the most famous Vespa in Tuscany! Anyway, you can't talk,' said Filippo to Roccia, pretending to be offended. 'You've got pig's ears on your helmet!'

Our food arrived, served on paper plates and tasting distinctly of pine-cone smoke. Roccia had finished his food and was hungrily eyeing ours. I said I'd have to get something tacky, a little touch of *cugi*-ness, for my Vespa.

'You already have,' piped up Marco. 'Your Maria. That's pretty *cugi*.'

I'd bought a Mary fridge magnet from Saint Mary's Cathedral in Sydney and had put it on the bike, just above the speedometer. I had hoped she would bring me good luck and protection on the trip, which I guess she had.

'But you need to get a new saint,' said Marco. 'One who hasn't been worn out by too many requests. Someone like Padre Pio.'

Marco reasoned that because Padre Pio was a new saint – the Pope had only canonised him a few months before – he still had 'much strength'. He wasn't as over-worked as the old saints.

It was an interesting concept, saints getting shagged out from being overtaxed by worshippers. I asked Marco if he had a biblical reference for it.

'Oh no!' he said with a grin. 'But it is this way, I swear!'

Praying for miracles is a strong tradition in Italy. During the recent World Cup in Japan and Korea, the Italian soccer player Francesco Totti poured holy water over his fingers from a small phial whenever he took a corner. And the Italian manager admitted he had prayed to the Almighty to get Italy into the quarter-finals. Of course, whether this was genuine Christian faith or just old-fashioned southern European super-stition was a matter for debate. Orazio Petrosillo, the well-known Italian Vaticanologist (now that's a job title!), wrote in the Roman daily, *Il Messaggero*, that praying for a miracle was a throwback to paganism.

Everyone at the table that night disagreed. 'But God reserves special favours for us,' said Filippo, only half-joking. 'Look at our countryside, look at our food. Look at our *women*!'

He made this last comment as an old woman, loaded up with plates *of spaghetti alla pignola*, tottered past. Everyone laughed, and it wasn't long before the con-versation turned to breasts – well, the fact that in Livorno the voluptuous curved cowls at the back of Vespas are called *puppa*, which is slang for breasts.

'I would have thought they were more like a woman's backside,' I said. 'I mean, they *are* at the back of the bike.'

'That's what the guys in Rome call them,' said Roccia. '*Chiappe* – buttocks!'

'They call them *polmone* [lungs] in Lucca,' said Roccia's girlfriend. 'Can you believe how uptight those guys are there?'

The conversation confirmed something I'd always suspected. Vespas were distinctly feminine. The very name ends in an 'a', the signifier in the Italian language that the object is feminine. And there is something vaguely sexual about a Vespa's soft, curvaceous lines and pinched waistline.

After we finished our meals Filippo insisted we looked at San Piero a Grado. It stood floodlit, maybe 300 metres away, on the other side of a field where a band was playing songs that only old folk and young children felt compelled to dance to. Filippo said it was built on the spot where Saint Peter first set foot on Italian soil in AD 42, and it featured frescoes by Deodati Orlandi detailing the life of the saint. The sea was over 6 kilometres away, and Roccia joked that it must have taken a miracle for Saint Peter to step ashore here.

'No!' said Filippo. 'The River Arno used to flow into

the sea here. It's just that centuries of silt deposits have moved the shoreline.'

The history lesson over, we retired to a shack nearby that happened to be a bar. It was the only place near the festival that sold alcohol – the festival itself was strictly a family affair – and it was jammed solid with folk looking for something a little stronger than pine-nut flavoured cordial. It looked like we would have to leave, until Roccia sauntered up to one table and glared at its occupants. They quickly skolled their drinks and left.

He called us over, laughing.

'He's really just a big pussy cat,' his girlfriend said, pinching his cheek.

Marco ordered *ponce* for everyone and they were brought to us on a battered metal tray by a waiter who looked harried and exhausted.

'Ahhh, *ponce*!' said Marco, knocking it back immediately and ordering another one before the waiter had a chance to leave.

It was the sort of Italian evening I had dreamt of when I was a teenager stranded in Sydney's western suburbs. The company was as lively and high-spirited as I had imagined too. But after I finished my *ponce* I made my excuses to leave. I had to get back to Lucca that night. It was the last of the nights I'd paid for. If I didn't get back in time I probably would find my belongings tossed out on the streets.

I thanked Marco and Filippo for an 'interesting' forty-eight hours and said I'd call them once Sally arrived.

I staggered into the hostel at midnight just as they were locking it up for the night.

'Where have you been for the last two days?' hissed one of the Perth moustache blokes when I got back into the dorm. 'We were going to send out a search party for you!'

'I'll tell you in the morning,' I whispered.

After the two unexpected days I'd just had I don't think they would have had much luck finding me. Unless, of course, Italian search parties bypass police stations and hospitals and head straight to pine-nut festivals and *ponce* bars.

CHAPTER TEN

Pisa

Kinder Surprise Toy: Cowboy Spinning a Lasso
(K02-090)

When I first set eyes on my Vespa in Milan, Gianni had told me the reason the engine was at the back of the bike on the right-hand side was to counterbalance the weight of the legs of female passengers riding side-saddle on the other. While this explanation seemed to have more than a whiff of urban myth to me – the bicycle-style passenger seat on Sophia would be painfully uncomfortable if you were sitting sideways – it underlined a fundamental truth about Vespas: the joy of riding one was meant to be a joy to be shared.

It's a message that Piaggio were not backward in promoting. Advertising for Vespas initially emphasised the bike's affordability and highlighted the company's radical easy-payment plan. But as post-war Europe became more affluent the message changed. Vespa posters started showing young, happy couples doing romantic and exciting things on their ever-faithful Vespas. Once for families, who clambered aboard six at a time, Vespas were now for lovers.

Him, her and the Vespa. It was a bizarre love triangle that Piaggio promoted by producing a series of post-cards for lovers to send each other from all over Europe. They depicted couples in romantic situations on their Vespas, and while they appear twee today they were phenomenally popular back then. A card featuring a suave young couple parked beside the running track at the empty Olympic stadium in Rome, for example, was one of the most-sent postcards in Italy in 1964.

The time had come for me to share. I didn't have plans to take Sally to the Olympic stadium in Rome during her time in Italy. I didn't have plans to take her to any stadium, actually. But I must admit I did have a series of Vespa postcard-type snapshots in my mind that I hoped would play out over the two weeks of her visit. Sally always wore a scarf and cat's-eye sunglasses in them. And, bizarrely, I had the ability to play the double bass. But while those elements were definitely far-fetched I hoped the parts that saw us riding past fields of sunflowers, eating fine food and spending the odd night or two in an old stone villa wouldn't be.

Sally was flying into Pisa, and as soon as I knew what day she was arriving I went online and booked accommodation for the first two nights. I found a four-star hotel, the Hotel Villa Kinzica, and while it was more expensive than I would have liked it was inside the old city walls and, according to the listing, each room had a view of the Leaning Tower.

The email confirmation I received after making the booking said that I could check into the room at eleven on the day of Sally's arrival, so I presented myself at the front desk only a minute or two past the hour. I was thrilled by the hotel's location. It was in a small piazza adjacent to Campo dei Miracoli, the grassy square that is home to the cathedral, baptistery and tower. The tower was barely 100 metres away, yet a combination of ridiculously tiny lanes and severe parking restrictions kept the area remarkably free of tourist coaches and tourists. Not that that was a problem riding a Vespa. I was able to ride Sophia right to the door and park her beside the pot plants that marked the perimeter of the hotel's *al fresco* restaurant.

Now, I don't know when the Hotel Villa Kinzica was awarded its four stars, but judging by the décor it had been some time back in the 1960s. In its heyday it would have been quite swish but, let's face it, the time for velvet wallpaper and floral-patterned carpet has passed.

At least, I *think* it was floral-patterned carpet. It was so threadbare I couldn't be sure, and it looked like it harboured DNA samples of every single guest that had ever stayed there. Even the uniforms of the cleaning staff looked like they had been passed down through the generations. I hoped things would get better when I got to the room, but it was small and poky, with an air-conditioning system that pushed out air so stale it was probably from the 1960s too. Worse, the double bed was simply two single beds pushed up against each other, with a set of double sheets valiantly trying to hold them together.

It did have a view of the Leaning Tower. Not of the *entire* tower, mind you – just the part that managed to peek above the Cyprus pine planted outside the window. It wasn't quite the view I had imagined – in my mind's eye there was a balcony, not just a window. But if I moved the writing table to the other side of the room we would be able to sip Camparis and soak up the view. We'd get a crick in our neck doing it, but we could do it.

I had five hours to kill before Sally's plane arrived and I was at a loss. The room had a TV but there is only so much Italian television you can watch before you become convinced that it is perfectly normal for female contestants to flash their breasts in the middle of a game show. I didn't want to go sightseeing around Pisa, either. I wanted it to be the first place that Sally and I looked at together. Instead, I decided to get some supplies from the Carrefour hypermarket I'd seen on the edge of town as I made my way into Pisa from Lucca.

Carrefour is a French company with stores in over thirty countries. On their website they claim to have invented the concept of hypermarkets, opening the first one in Sainte-Geneviève-des-bois in 1963. While that might be a touch of Gallic hyperbole – I can't believe the Americans didn't come up with the idea of a store the size of a suburb first – Carrefour's success in Italy is considerable. At the end of 2002 they boasted 203 supermarkets, eighty-six convenience stores, twelve cash-and-carries and thirty-four hypermarkets. If the number of cars fighting for parking spaces at the one in Pisa was anything to go by, they were doing rather well for themselves.

As a scooter rider I didn't have to worry about such tiresome things as finding a parking spot. I simply parked Sophia on the footpath near the entrance door like every other scooter rider in Pisa. There seemed to be a competition going on to see who could park closest to the sliding glass doors without triggering the automatic opening mechanism. Try as I might, I couldn't better the effort of the owner of an old green Cosa. He'd parked his bike within a millimetre of the range of the electric door's eye.

While the motor scooter parking arrangements gave the Carrefour a distinctly Italian ambience, it ended abruptly once I entered the store. With its harsh neon lighting and insipid piped music it was like every other hypermarket in the world. More disturbingly, the shelves were loaded with the same products on offer back home in Australia. There was Clairol botanics shampoo and Kellogg's cornflakes and bottles of wine from south-eastern Australia. I wandered up and down the generously spaced aisles looking for something I couldn't buy back in Sydney and was largely thwarted.

Then I reached the deli section. It took up at least a third of the store's floor space, and offered all kinds of cheeses and small goods, including a staggering fifty-seven different types of ham. It attracted most of the store's customers, too, and they lined the serving counters five deep, jostling and brawling, trying to get the attention of the girls serving, and ignoring the stands dispensing numbers that were supposed to indicate who was next. I took one and waited, but when it became apparent that the staff paid as much attention to the system as the customers I tossed it aside and joined the scrum.

Loaded up with Parma ham, bocconcini cheese, tomatoes, and a loaf of crusty bread, I wove my way towards the checkout counters, stopping briefly to pick up a jar of artichoke hearts in another corner of the extensive deli section. I also grabbed some candles, which I hoped would miraculously transform the ambience of the hotel room or at least hide its deficiencies. As I picked up a couple of Kinder Surprises – one of them surely had a green Vespa inside – I noticed the other distinctly Italian thing about the Carrefour hypermarket in Pisa: Italian parents allowed their children to run riot.

Actually, that's not strictly correct. They allowed their young *boys* to run riot. The girls stood close to their mother's side and didn't utter a word while their brothers ran up and down aisles scattering packets of cereal in their wake. The naughtiest would deliberately spill milk on the floor and then hide behind the Cheerios to watch people slip over. Meanwhile, their mothers and grandmothers smiled at them indulgently. Astonishingly, the supermarket staff simply walked behind the boys with a mop, cleaning up after them and suppressing what I would think would be a natural urge to stick a mop handle up their annoying little arses.

It was worse at the checkout. Although there were enough checkout counters to serve several coachloads of customers only five of them were open and the queues stretched back to the deli and around to the freezer section. If Italian boys had trouble amusing themselves as their mothers walked up and down aisles they were positively bored furious at having to wait in line. The boy with his mother behind me decided to pass the time by writhing around the floor in a tantrum.

It wasn't the screaming and wailing that bothered me. I'd travelled on enough buses in Indonesia while being forced to listen to the screeching heavy metal music favoured by their drivers to be able to block out even the most offensive of sounds. But this kid was thrashing around on the floor like an epileptic and every time he kicked out he kicked me. It was only a light kick, but I knew it was coming and somehow that made it worse. I tensed for the blow whenever he choked back his sobs and let out a piercing wail.

If I'd behaved as badly in public when I was a kid I would have been grabbed by the scruff of the neck and *made* to stand up. My mother wouldn't have walloped me – *not in public*. But she'd have made it exceedingly clear, and not necessarily in words, that I was in for the hiding of my life once we got home. This kid's mother and grandmother looked at him adoringly and offered him a chocolate.

As I was placing my purchases on the conveyor belt the kid kicked out again and caught me awkwardly on the ankle. It hurt, and although I should have bit my lip and suffered in silence, I snapped at the woman to keep her bloody kid under control. I said it in English but it was obvious from my tone what I had said. The mother pulled her brat close to her as if I was going to hurt *him*. The checkout girl stopped scanning and glared at me. And the other people in the queue started whispering among themselves like I was a murderer on the run from the law. They were still whispering and pointing as I left the store.

I arrived at Pisa's Galileo Galilei airport an hour earlier than I should have and found that the flight Sally was on was already indefinitely delayed. As I stood at the counter in a futile attempt to find out what was happening, Sally texted me to say she had boarded the plane but it was still sitting on the tarmac at Stansted. She texted me an hour later to say they were still on the runway.

Her plane finally arrived in Pisa just before midnight, close to five hours later than it should have. Sally walked into the arrival hall in remarkably good spirits and toting an incredibly small bag. We hugged and I asked her where her baggage was.

'You told me to pack lightly!' she said, pretending to be miffed but secretly pleased I had expected her to bring more.

I'd been quite adamant about the size of the bag, actually. Indeed, every time I texted Sally, emailed her or spoke to her on the phone I'd stressed just how important it was that she brought a small and compact bag. Sophia was an old bike and I wasn't sure how she would cope with two people on board, let alone two people and an awful lot of luggage. To Sally's credit, she'd resisted the natural urge to bring a huge bag just to spite me for being such a nagger. I knew then that the following two weeks were going to be okay.

At night Pisa is a surprisingly pretty city. The handsome buildings that line the River Arno, which appear a little grubby during the day, in the evenings are awash in light that conceals their flaws. The ruins of the ancient city walls that surround the old part of the city are floodlit, too, and the cobbled streets that are busy and congested during the day are empty and deserted.

It would be lovely from a tourist coach, but on a Vespa, in the crisp evening air, with a girl on the back, her arms wrapped tightly around my waist, it was extra special.

Instead of parking in front of the hotel I continued 100 metres to the Campo dei Miracoli and stopped in front of the Leaning Tower. The whole area was deserted and swallows wheeled between the cathedral and the tower, catching bugs attracted to the lights. I turned to speak to Sally. She was staring, stunned, her mouth wide open.

'It's outrageous!' she said. 'I know it's the *Leaning* Tower of Pisa but I didn't think it leant that much!'

The hotel's restaurant was closed so we had a candle-lit picnic on the bed, feasting on the stuff I had bought at Carrefour earlier that day. I'd bought two Kinder Surprises, one of which I was sure would hold the green Vespa. Sally got a cowboy that spun a lasso as you wheeled him along. I got another bloody Smurf, this time wielding a tennis racquet.

Before we went to sleep, we rearranged the bed and slept with our feet near the headboard. That way, with the shutters open, we could just spot the top of the tower peeping above the pine tree.

We slept in late the next morning and began sightseeing around Pisa just as everything was closing for the midday siesta. Pisa is a university town and it has that certain buzz that many student towns have. The cafés were somehow more lively than the ones in Lucca. And the clothes in the stores were younger and funkier.

There was also a hell of a lot more motor scooters. For a student, a Vespa still represents the most affordable way to get around. When in 1963 the Italian government brought in a law that anyone over fourteen could ride a moped with an engine capacity up to 50cc Piaggio produced the Vespa 50. Affectionately known as the *Vesperino*, the little Vespa, it was an instant hit among young people, and over 23,000 were sold in its first year of production alone. Teenagers bought them because they were cheap, stylish and fun.

Sally and I wandered up Corso Italia, peering into the shops that were already closed, and checked out Santa Maria della Spina, the tiny church bristling with miniature Gothic spires and supposedly home to one of the thorns from Christ's crown. We swung by Piazza dei Cavalieri, an exuberant black and white building with designs that had been scratched into the wet plaster as it was built. But like every visitor to Pisa we always ended up back at the tower and the Campo dei Miracoli.

I liked the area around the Campo dei Miracoli. Not only are the buildings exceedingly beautiful – Carrara marble has rarely been fashioned into anything so exquisite – but they are also surrounded by vast grassy areas that are full of people. It gives the whole complex a lively, almost family feel. Kids run about. Couples canoodle. And backpackers picnic. Even the crappy souvenir stalls that line the road appear more festive. I walked past one playing Michael Jackson and did a moonwalk and the guy joined in, doing a much better version on the footpath in front of his stall.

The most astonishing thing I learnt that day was that *all* the buildings on the Campo dei Miracoli lean, including the cathedral and baptistery. Apparently the sandy, silty subsoil that reaches a depth of 40 metres wasn't exactly the best foundation to build on. But none of the buildings tilt as severely as the Torre Pendente – the Leaning Tower.

Construction on the tower began in 1173 and by the time artisans and masons had finished the third storey the tower was already leaning considerably. Time out was called and for the next hundred years Pisa's finest engineers considered the problem. In 1272 a new band of artisans and masons decided to take what was effectively the 'banana' approach. They simply kept going and compensated for the lean by gradually building straight up from the third storey on, giving the building a slight but distinctly noticeable banana curve.

That the 'banana' approach has not won much credibility in the world of architecture and building today is probably because the tower in Pisa continued to lean anyway, tilting a further 1 millimetre each year. By 1990 the tilt had become critical and the tower was closed to the public.

With the livelihood of thousands of souvenir sellers at stake, the government in Rome assembled a panel of experts to come up with a solution. Some suggested placing 1000 tonnes of lead ingots on the northern side to counterbalance the lean on the southern side. Others suggested securing steel cables around the third storey and then attaching it by cables to surrounding buildings. One of the most radical plans was to knock the tower down and replace it with a holographic representation of what had once stood there. Okay, I made that one up but, you've got to admit, it's no more ridiculous than the steel-cable idea.

Having said that, it was the steel-cable approach that the government finally settled upon. With the tower thus held in place, engineers dug out 70 tonnes of soil from beneath the northern side, rectifying the lean by a whacking 43.8 centimetres! The tower was re-opened with great fanfare in December 2001, and experts are convinced that the miniature alabaster leaning tower souvenir industry is secure for at least another 300 years.

Since the tower has been reopened the number of visitors at any time has been restricted and you have to book a ticket ahead of time. I'd bought our tickets the day before, between my visit to Carrefour and going out to the airport, and already most of the nominated time slots were full. I got two tickets for the 5.30 pm climb, and we reached the top just as the sun was casting a golden glow over the cathedral below us. Not being a great fan of heights Sally had a quick look at the view – not letting go of the railing for a second – and then quickly made her way down again.

I had arranged to have dinner with Marco and Filippo that night. The plan was to meet at Marco's workshop at seven. After our climb we quickly showered and set off for Livorno. We were making good time, too, until Sophia started backfiring loudly as we passed the American base at Camp Darby.

It struck me that a heavily fortified American army base with trigger-happy guards was not the most fortuitous place to be making large explosive noises. But the more I eased off the throttle the more Sophia backfired. It got to the stage where the engine gave up altogether and the bike was being propelled by the explosion of the backfire alone. We made it past the army base unscathed and, eventually, at a grand speed of 5 kilometres an hour, into the centre of Livorno itself. At the set of traffic lights in front of the Hotel Gran Duca, still a kilometre or two from the workshop, Sophia expired.

I rang Marco and within minutes he arrived in his Mini. Marco's Mini was British racing green and had a walnut dash, and he loved it almost as much as he loved his Vespas. In his workshop I'd seen a photo of him standing in front of it, looking very British in a tweed jacket and scarf and with a basset hound that he'd borrowed from a friend.

Marco immediately diagnosed Sophia's problem as the points. He produced a pair of surgical gloves and a screwdriver from the Mini's glove box and instructed me to take off the bike's cowl. I felt like a nurse assisting in an operation and watched in admiration as Marco deftly adjusted the points with the screwdriver. Within moments he was finished and I put the cowl back on like I was sewing up after an op. Marco instructed me to kick-start Sophia. She started first time. Apparently the gap in the points had widened and Marco had simply tweaked them back to where they were supposed to be.

'Now follow me,' said Marco with a grin. 'We're late!'

I'd expected to be eating in Livorno, maybe revisiting some of the places we'd been on my first night in the city. But not one to repeat himself, Filippo had organised a table in a famous little restaurant in

Fauglia, a town in the Tuscan hills about 25 kilometres out of Livorno.

We followed Marco and his Mini through the industrial outskirts of Livorno and into the countryside. The road followed an old stone aqueduct and dipped gently through rolling fields dotted with giant wheels of harvest hay or of row upon row of sunflowers that dipped their heads towards the setting sun.

The early evening air was cool and fresh on our faces and Sally squeezed me around the waist then leant forward to speak. 'This is beautiful!' she shouted, in an attempt to be heard over the noise of the wind. 'It is just like I imagined it would be.'

After half an hour we turned off the road that followed the aqueduct and on to another one that wound its way up a hill towards Fauglia. As Tuscan towns go, Fauglia was nothing special. In fact, with its nondescript buildings and extraordinary number of solariums, it reminded me an awful lot of Broni. But after we parked the bike and followed Marco down a small alley between two buildings to La Gattaiola I could see why Filippo had brought us there. The tables were set on a terrace with a pergola covered in wisteria and overlooking a beautiful valley. It was one of the most tranquil and soothing views I had ever seen.

Filippo was already sitting at the table with Michela. She worked in the marketing department of Piaggio and was perhaps his most serious girlfriend.

'You are late!' he smiled, pointing to an opened bottle of wine. 'We started without you!'

The restaurant was owned by Francesco Gattaiola, an ex-boxer who'd made quite a name for himself in the mid 1980s with his devastating right hook. He was small and compact with a flat nose, and wore a tight black T-shirt that showed he was still in good shape.

'He was probably a fly-weight,' said Sally, revealing a previously undisclosed expertise in the sweet science of boxing.

Filippo ordered the food. His banter with Francesco indicated that he was obviously a regular and would know which dishes were the best. I meant to make a note of what we ate in my notepad, if only to be able to order with confidence at restaurants later in the trip, but I got so caught up in the conversations, the arguments, the joking and the general bonhomie of the evening that I didn't jot down a word. I know the food was excellent, though. I could tell from the look on Sally's face whenever she took a mouthful.

Between *primi piatti* and the main course, Francesco gave Sally and me a tour of his establishment. The kitchen and the main dining area of the restaurant was set in a building centuries old that had an underground cellar with stone walls lined with suitably dusty bottles of wine. The walls of the dining room were lined with old black and white photos of the town and the surrounding area. And there was a wooden bowl full of freshly picked wild mushrooms. For a battle-scarred pugilist, Francesco was quite the aesthete.

After the meal we followed Filippo in his Méhari until he pointed out the road back to Pisa. Since Marco adjusted Sophia's points she had not missed a beat, and as we approached Pisa, the strong farm smells intensified by the darkness, I felt a thrill in the pit of my stomach. This was exactly how I had hoped my Italian Vespa adventure would unfold. I was riding through Tuscany on a beautiful old Vespa with an equally beautiful woman on the back. I was dining on exquisite food in a hidden gem of a restaurant not mentioned in guidebooks. And I was socialising with cool new Italian friends.

When Sally squeezed my waist and rested her head on my shoulder I knew she was impressed, too.

CHAPTER ELEVEN

Montopoli in Val d'Arno

Kinder Surprise Toy: Brown Dog in a Yellow Basket
(K02-071)

The heavens opened about 5 kilometres into our journey to Florence and my good standing with Sally vanished as rapidly as the sun. I'd only brought one set of wet-weather gear, you see, and it was packed at the bottom of my bag.

In my defence I'd like to point out that I'd been in Italy forty-three days and it hadn't rained once. I'd travelled close to 700 kilometres and the only moisture I'd felt was the sweat from my brow and the remains of the bugs that committed suicide on my shirt as I rode along. Italy was in the middle of a drought. Every evening the television news broadcast pictures of people in the south of the country lining up to get water from a water truck. How was I to know that it would tip down on the day Sally and I set off to ride around Tuscany on a motor scooter?

That was the thing with motor scooters. You were exposed to the elements. Which was all well and good when the elements were in a benign mood, when the sun tickled your skin and there wasn't a cloud in the sky. But when the elements turned nasty and the day turned grey and wet like this one, well, you were stuffed.

Back in the 1950s Piaggio attempted to resolve the problem by attaching a curved canopy from the front of the bike to the back. It was a precursor to the idea used now by the new BMW motor scooter, the C1. The good folk at Piaggio, however, had the sense to see that it was eminently impractical and decidedly lacking in style. They offered Vespa owners a windscreen, instead, and for the colder months a piece of canvas that attached to the front shield and covered the bottom half of your body, keeping your legs warm. If you wanted any more protection than that you bought a raincoat.

Sophia was as unimpressed by the rain as Sally was, and she spluttered and coughed as I desperately looked for somewhere to shelter. In a fit of spite she began back-firing again, startling a flock of birds sheltering in a tree into taking flight. It was clearly the points again and I nursed Sophia through the inclement weather as best I could until Cascina. Here, still only 11 kilometres from Pisa, I found an Agip petrol station that had an awning we could wait under until the rain passed.

It was Sunday so the petrol station was closed. If my journey in Italy had taught me one thing it was that the working hours of an Italian petrol station attendant were a thing to envy. They put in an average of six hours each weekday and didn't bother getting out of bed on the weekend. Sally got all excited when she noticed a small mechanic's shop attached to the petrol station but by bitter experience I knew that any mechanic would be home in bed as well.

I found a dry spot under the awning and pulled off the cowl protecting the engine. Consulting my Haynes manual I found the section on points in chapter three: Ignition System. I gained access to them through the slots in the rotor as the book instructed, and set about adjusting the points on a forty-year-old Vespa for the first time in my life.

Sensing that these things can take time, Sally set up a mini-picnic on one of our towels, pulling her wet clothes away from her skin to air them and scoffing the Vegemite and biscuit snack she'd brought over for me from the Australia Shop in London. All I had to do was check that the gap between the contact points was between 0.3 and 0.5 millimetres with a feeler gauge and we'd be on our way. The trouble was, I didn't *have* a feeler gauge.

On the night in Livorno that Sophia had broken down in front of the Hotel Gran Duca, Marco had simply adjusted the points by sight. He'd worked on so many Vespas he could tell when the gap was - correct just by looking at it. Me? I had no idea what 0.3 millimetres looked like. Up until that moment in my life I'd had no reason to know. I decided to ask Sally. As the old joke goes, women are much more accurate with measurements, anyway.

'Does that look like 0.3 millimetres to you?' I asked, hoping she realised it was the gap I was talking about.

Sally shrugged her shoulders and went back to reading *marie claire*. It was obvious I'd have to adjust the points by trial and error. If Sophia started and ran smoothly, chances were the gap was 0.3 millimetres. If she didn't, it wasn't, and I'd have to start all over again.

Eventually I got Sophia to start and when I turned the throttle she revved smoothly, without a stutter or backfire. That lasted for 5 kilometres, until the rain returned, and she began backfiring again. The gap between the points had widened and I would have to adjust it again. I apologised to Sally for ruining her annual holiday.

She was very understanding. 'Don't worry about it,' she said. 'I'm used to it. My dad was a mechanic.'

Sally had spent a good deal of her teens in Lincoln reading books beside broken-down vehicles while her dad had his head under the bonnet. Strange noises and niggly problems don't always reveal themselves on a ramp in the workshop so he'd often take a car for a drive to see what was wrong with it. More often than not the problem revealed itself in the middle of nowhere on the road to Branston. In some ways Sally had been in training for this moment all her life.

I was able to get Sophia started again fairly quickly, but it was clear we weren't going to make it to Florence that day. We had been travelling for close to three hours and had covered a grand total of 16 kilometres. The weather was still miserable and the road we were on, the S67, seemed to pass through one depressing industrial town after another. We decided to take the next turnoff and look for somewhere to stay in the surrounding countryside – an area of farms and hilltop towns that looked altogether more alluring. Unfortunately, the turnoff I chose put us on the motorway to Florence.

I didn't realise we were heading for the motorway until it was too late and we were puttering on the slip road towards an unbroken line of vehicles zipping along at high speed. It was illegal for me to be on that road with a motorcycle with an engine capacity less than 150cc, but breaking the law was the last thing on my mind. We were sucked into the outside lane and buffeted by the wind drag of passing vehicles like a tiny boat tossed on wild seas.

I hadn't ridden on a road this busy before. Every vehicle on the motorway seemed to be travelling at warp speed and rain had made the road slippery and treacherous. Semi-trailers passed at such great speeds, and so close I began to suspect they were deliberately trying to knock us off. I held on for dear life, screaming 'Fuuuuuuuuuuuucccckkkk!' until we came to the first turnoff 8 kilometres along. It was one of the most frightening experiences of my life.

The freeway spat us out near Montopoli in Val d'Arno, a medieval town sitting on a hill overlooking the Arno Valley. The town climbed up the hillside like a red terracotta snake and the surrounding hills were dotted with villas and olive farms. We spotted a sign pointing towards an *agriturismo* (farm-stay) a couple of kilometres away, and decided to see if they had a room. The gap between the contact points must have shifted because Sophia began spluttering again.

The road leading to the *agriturismo* was dirt and cut through a forest that dripped heavily with rain. The *agriturismo* itself sat high on a hill among olive trees, at the top of a road that wound its way up the side of the hill like a Himalayan path. Sophia refused to go up it and after one last petulant 'pop', she died altogether.

The rain was steady now and as I tried to adjust the points, Sally stood beside me in my wet-weather gear, still wearing her helmet in an attempt to keep her head dry. I suggested she continue on to see if the *agriturismo* had a room, and with shoulders slumped she trudged off up the hill. She had sixteen days' annual leave and I'm sure this was not how she had imagined spending them. Twenty minutes later she returned, still wearing the helmet, to say they had a room for €50, including dinner. I told her to take it and she set off up the hill again. I finally got Sophia to start soon after and rode her up the hill, arriving the same time Sally did.

The Azienda Agrituristica Montalto was a working winery and olive farm built on the site of a castle that was destroyed during a battle between the Ghibellines from Pisa and the Guelphs from Florence in 1355. Our room was in the old eighteenth-century farmhouse, on the top floor and in the north-eastern corner of the building. It boasted terracotta tiles on the floor, exposed wooden beams and a bed that looked like it had been carved from a giant tree. The farmhouse was at the highest point of the farm and when we threw open the shutters we were greeted by a magnificent view across the olive groves to Montopoli, on another ridge but with a valley in between. Because ours was a corner room there was another window, which looked back towards the Garfagnana, the Apennines and the Apuane Alps. It was everything I'd hoped my first *agriturismo* would be. And I'd never have found it if Sophia hadn't played up.

I spread out my Michelin map and found Montopoli in Val d'Arno. I noticed with alarm we were only 29 kilometres from Pisa and still a good 40 kilometres short of Florence.

While Sally took a hot shower I went downstairs to speak to the woman who ran the place. She had a rather brusque manner, and when I asked her if there was someone on the farm who could look at Sophia and maybe fix the problem with the points, she shrugged her shoulders and grimaced.

'We have a mechanic in town who fixes our tractors and vehicles,' she said nonchalantly. 'I will call him tomorrow.'

Dinner that night was a simple stew served with crusty bread and a complimentary bottle of white wine served in a dining hall with vaulted ceilings and whitewashed walls. The wine was produced on the farm, as were the olives served as an entree and the olive oil presented in plain glass containers to pour on our bread. All the dogs that lived on the farm sat at a glass door leading out to a patio and took turns at sneaking in to beg for scraps.

The stew was very good, the sort of hearty food one needs after a day spent in the rain adjusting contact points. The wine was excellent, too, which shouldn't have surprised me in such a renowned wine-growing area but for some reason did. (Thinking back it could have been the rudimentary label, featuring a hand-drawn picture of the farmhouse, that threw me.)

Sally took a thoughtful swig of the wine, rolled it around in her mouth and declared it had an apple flavour. 'It doesn't hit you until it's halfway down your throat,' she said. 'But it's definitely got a touch of the Granny Smiths.'

I must have looked shocked, because Sally felt compelled to explain. 'What?' she said throwing her hands up. 'Didn't I tell you that I'm very good at identifying the flavours produced by different grapes?'

Apparently it was a skill she'd picked up chaperoning authors. She was a publicist for a publisher in the UK and her job involved organising publication dinners and launches. She'd become quite adept at picking up good wines at good prices.

I took another sip, letting the wine slide down my throat slowly, and realised with a smile she was right. It *did* taste of apple.

I'm always envious of people with a good palate for wine. I have an excellent palate, too, but my skills lie in the less lofty world of colas. I can pick a Diet Coke within a split second and can distinguish a Pepsi from a Coke without even thinking. Sadly, I can also pick out lesser-known brands, such as Virgin Cola and Black & Gold Cola from IGA, in an instant, too. When Coca-Cola recently released Vanilla Coke in Australia I alarmed friends and acquaintances with my claim that it had a palate reminiscent of Zing Cola, an obscure brand from my childhood that my nanna used to buy because it cost less than 5 cents a can.

It rained through the night, at some points drumming so hard against the terracotta roof it woke us from our sleep. It was still hot, though, and the high level of humidity brought out a squadron of mosquitoes who promptly began to feast on Sally. She woke up the next morning spotted with red welts. Worse, she'd had an allergic reaction to the ant bites she'd got at the ex-boxer's restaurant in Fauglia and her right ankle had swollen to elephantine proportions.

The news about Sophia was not good, either. The mechanic from town visited and declared that a new set of points was needed. Apparently the person who had fitted the last set – that would be Giuseppe or his father in Ponte dell'Olio – forgot to lubricate the felt pad that rubbed against the flywheel. It had worn at such an angle that no matter how many times the gap was adjusted it would always be thrown out again very quickly.

The mechanic took Sophia away in a van, promising to call once he'd fitted her with a new set of points.

As the van drove away I realised just how much Sophia had allowed me to go wherever I pleased and do whatever I wanted to do. Instead of waiting for trains and buses I simply started her up and rode away. Instead of organising my itinerary around a Eurail pass I was able to discover hidden corners of Italy I didn't even know existed. In a word, she had given me freedom.

Which, in fact, was what had attracted me to Vespas when I was younger, more so than the pneumatic women who rode them in the movies. I spent my teens on a 5-acre farm on the outskirts of Sydney, 20 kilometres from the nearest train station. During the week there was the odd bus or two to Liverpool station, but on the weekend, if I wanted to go anywhere, I had to talk my dad into driving me. And once I got to the station I'd still have to wait for up to an hour for an old red rattler to take me into the city.

The rain continued to fall relentlessly. Sally and I lay on the bed in our room until lunchtime, listlessly staring out the window at the valley shrouded in mist, bored out of our minds. I know we shouldn't have been – the Montalto was quiet and peaceful and offered a great opportunity to just relax. But Sally was like me. She needed to be doing things. So we borrowed two umbrellas and set off into town.

The walk to Montopoli involved trundling down one hill and then struggling up another. The rain eased soon after we left and by the time we reached the outskirts of the town we had rolled up our umbrellas. I'd hoped to find a charming *osteria* to have lunch in but there wasn't one, so we whiled away the hours eating cheese and tomato rolls in the local bar. The bar also sold Kinder Surprises, and we bought two as a special treat. I got a dog in a yellow basket. Sally got a jigsaw, perhaps the most disappointing of the Kinder Surprise toys. The green Vespa remained as elusive as ever.

Sally wanted to get some antihistamine cream for her bites so we waited in the bar until the siesta was over and the local *farmacia* had opened. The female pharmacist didn't understand English and we couldn't find the appropriate term in our phrase book, so Sally lifted up her leg to show her. The pharmacist recoiled and exclaimed '*Mamma mia*!' before regaining enough of her professional composure to prod Sally's leg to see if it hurt. When Sally flinched she shook her head and prescribed a tube of cream. She was still shaking her head when we left the shop.

Late on the afternoon of our third day in Montopoli the mechanic rang to say that Sophia was fixed and ready to go. The mechanic's workshop was 15 kilometres away, in an industrial estate beside the freeway.

The cranky old farm-stay manager drove me there, sucking on a cigarette and not uttering a single word the entire way. When we arrived, the young mechanic apologised for taking so long, and when I asked how much I owed him he looked at the manager for a hint. She raised her eyebrows and he said €30, an extraordinarily low amount considering he had come out to the *agriturismo* to pick the bike up. I suspect the Montalto put a lot of business through him and expected a good deal for their guests in return.

I rode back to Montalto exhilarated, not just by the price but also by how well Sophia was going. She powered up the final steep ascent to the farmhouse like it was a gentle slope.

We set off for Florence the next morning just after breakfast. The sun was shining and both Sally and Sophia were in better spirits. The new set of points had made Sophia sparkier and livelier and the cream the pharmacist had given Sally had worked wonders on her leg. I set off towards Florence with a renewed sense of optimism that the worst was now behind us.

The S67 from Montopoli to Florence is not the most attractive route in Italy. In fact, I would almost go so far as to say it is one of its most horrible. It passes through the heart of the Pisa–Florence industrial conurbation and at times it is little more than a collection of factories, warehouses and junkyards. The traffic was the worst I'd seen, too, and although we were able to weave our way through, we still breathed in more noxious fumes than was advisable.

Three kilometres from Florence the road signs became confusing and we spent half an hour cruising through an industrial estate looking for the B-road into town. When we ended back at the Carrefour warehouse for the third time I decided enough was enough and turned onto the entrance ramp to the motorway. I'd rather have got a ticket for riding an underpowered motor scooter on a motorway than spend the night circling an industrial estate.

From the industrial estate the motorway had looked heavily congested. The traffic was at a standstill, caused perhaps by an accident up ahead, but the ramp we came up dumped us onto three empty lanes. About 500 metres down the road a police car came hurtling towards us, sirens blazing, but rather than stop it swerved around us, dramatically turning sideways to block any other vehicle from following us. Sally was convinced we were about to come upon a horrific accident, perhaps a limb or two strewn on the road. But all we got were three lanes of black-top, empty and silent, leading us all the way into the heart of Florence.

CHAPTER TWELVE

Florence

Kinder Surprise Toy: Spider with a Ladybird
(K02-075)

I'm going to go out on a limb here and admit that I don't actually *like* Florence. It's crowded, it's dirty and you get the distinct feeling it would be exactly the same even if the millions of tourists who squeeze into the city each year stopped turning up. I won't be popular saying it – there's probably already a contract out on my head, financed by the kind of people who can recite the entire script of *Room with a View* backwards – but I don't care. It has to be said.

There's just no sense of space. Take the Duomo, for example, or il Cattedrale di Santa Maria del Fiore to give it its proper name, smack bang in the centre of town and topped by the red-tiled dome that is to Florence what the Opera House is to Sydney. Here we have one of the most amazing buildings of the Renaissance, clad in white, green and pink Tuscan marble. It was designed by Brunelleschi to dwarf even the great buildings of ancient Rome and Greece, but you only have to walk 10 metres before you hit another building. The dome is the largest of its time built without scaffolding, but there's just no room to appreciate its size. And what little room that's there is filled with thousands of people lining up to get into the cathedral and just as many Senegalese hawkers trying to sell them fake Louis Vuitton handbags.

It's not until you step back from Florence, I think, that it reveals its beauty. You need to get up high somewhere, where you can get the big picture, an overview of that famous skyline dominated by the Duomo's dome. And far enough away so that the famous red terracotta tiles are like a blanket thrown over the city, hiding the filth and the crowds from view. Giardino di Boboli, the park on a hill just the other side of the Ponte Vecchio, can give you that perspective. But it's even better up in Fiesole, a town only 8 kilometres from Florence. It's high in the hills of the Mugello region, and has been a popular summer retreat for wealthy Florentines since the fifteenth century.

As we wound our way up the steep road that leads to the town you could see that the higher you went the higher the incomes of the people who lived in the villas there. It was neater, cleaner and more immaculate. The view across the valley to the city and the dome of the Duomo, the River Arno snaking beside it, got much better, too. I don't think Sophia was impressed, though. She had to really struggle up the final stretch of road and arrived at Piazza Mino da Fiesole wheezing like an asthmatic.

We had come to Fiesole because I had bought tickets for an opera that was being staged in the old Roman amphitheatre there. The town has been presenting operas in the Roman ruins each summer for the past fifty-five years and this year they were highlighting the work of local Tuscan boy Puccini. I'd remembered Sally saying once that she liked the music in *La Bohème* – I think she'd heard it in the movie *Moonstruck*, which starred Cher and a younger Nicolas Cage – so I thought I'd earn some relationship brownie points by taking her to another Puccini opera, this time set in a gorgeous outdoor setting. The Fiesole Opera Festival wasn't doing *La Bohème* this year so I picked up a couple of tickets for *Tosca* instead.

I would have earned a whole heap more brownie points if I'd been sensible enough to book a room in Fiesole ahead of time as well. The Opera Festival meant that all the hotels in the centre of town were full and we had to venture out along the ridge towards Montereggi to find somewhere to stay. It was a tight and narrow road with fish-eye mirrors set on buildings so that drivers can spot vehicles coming in the opposite direction. Some sections were so tight that a couple of times cars had to stop and back up to get around. On Sophia it wasn't a problem. In fact it was actually a lot of fun.

A woman at the ATP Tourist office in Fiesole had given me a map showing all the hotels and *agriturismi* in the area and had circled one place, the one-star Villa Baccano, as a hotel within our budget. When the manager opened the door, however, he looked me up and down once and said they were full. They weren't, of course. Most of the room keys were hanging on a rack on the wall behind the reception desk and the gravel carpark was empty. The manager just didn't like the look of me.

Okay, I was in a state. I'd been riding in traffic for most of the day and I was tired and dirty. I tried letting him see I was riding on an old Vespa – it had worked a treat on my journey so far – but Sally blocked Sophia from view and looked a right mess, too. But that was no excuse for this guy's rudeness. We're not talking about the Ritz here. This was a lousy one-star establishment on the outskirts of Fiesole that could do with a lick of paint and, if the rustling in the bushes was anything to go by, a visit from the local exterminator.

My first impulse was to ring the doorbell again and give the manager a piece of my mind when he opened it.

My second impulse was to ring the doorbell and hide, and keep doing it for at least a couple of hours. My third impulse was to fire-bomb the place. My fourth, and one I am still working on, was to go off and become exceedingly rich, buy the place and then kick him out on his arse. But I didn't act on any of them that day. I simply jumped back on Sophia and headed further out along the road to Montereggi. I did do a bit of a doughnut on the gravel drive as we left but it was nothing he couldn't have remedied with a broom and some effort.

It was hard to stay angry riding through the countryside. The vista of valleys, cypresses, stone walls and villas looked like it been untouched for centuries, as if the folk who lived around here realised once it was perfect and left it alone. Within moments my mood had lightened and any thoughts of fire-bombing the Villa Baccano were banished from my mind.

Instead of continuing along the road to Montereggi I turned off at Monte Fanna, hoping we would find a room in an *agriturismo* or villa here while we were still relatively close to Fiesole. Just past a small chapel the road went up at a steep angle and after making a half-hearted attempt to negotiate it Sophia refused to go any further. I changed down through the gears until she was in first, but even then she didn't have enough power to conquer the rise, and she came to a stop with an undignified 'urrggh'. I applied the brakes but they weren't up to the task and the bike started rolling backwards. I shouted for Sally to jump off before I lost control of the bike.

Sally is quite slight – the scales barely reach 52 kilos when she is on them – but once she jumped off I was able to coax Sophia up the hill to a point where the inclination wasn't so steep. As Sally struggled up the hill to catch up with us, Sophia purred contentedly, as if nothing was wrong.

'I'm sure that bloody bike did that on purpose,' gasped Sally when she finally arrived. 'Lazy cow!'

From that point on the road continued at an incline that Sophia found more acceptable and soon we came upon a sign for an *agriturismo* called Villa Le Capanne. It featured a picture of a bed and pointed down a dirt road that quickly disappeared into a thick forest. It was a little further away from Fiesole than I would have liked – I didn't particularly fancy coming back all this way in the dark after the opera the next night. But it was getting late and we needed to find somewhere to stay.

The road turned out to be more of a path. We followed it towards a valley through stands of pine trees and across small streams. Just on dusk we spotted the villa, an old two-storey building with smoking chimneys, sitting lonely on a hill without another skerrick of civilisation for miles.

The entrance gate for Villa Le Capanne was electronic, with a video security camera, and was 500 metres from the villa. It was the sort of thing that Sting might have at the entrance to his Tuscan villa and Sally and I looked at each other and agreed that the villa was probably way out of our price range. If the guy at the Villa Baccano hadn't liked the look of us then these people were going to hate us.

As I went to turn Sophia around and head back to the main road there was a clunk and the whirr of an electric motor and the gate slid open. The intercom remained silent. I'd hoped at least that a distorted, crackling voice would ask us who we were and demand to know what we were doing there.

'Well,' said Sally. 'We may as well go and have a look at how the other half live!'

The other half, it turned out, didn't live quite as well as we expected. On closer inspection the villa was in poor repair, the gardens overgrown and the outdoor furniture faded and worn. A Russian woman in her late thirties wearing bookish glasses came out to greet us with a weary smile that suggested we would turn around and leave like everyone else.

Her name was Svetlana and she had come to Italy when she married the farmer who owned the villa. 'I like your motor scooter,' she said in a thick Eastern European accent. 'Ve 'ave ones just like it in Rooo-shia.'

In Russian the Vespa was called the *Vyatka* and was first seen by the Moscow public at the Agricultural and Industrial Fair of June 1957. It was presented as a 'glorious Soviet invention' but was in fact an exact copy of a Vespa 150GS, smuggled into the country and mimeographed piece by piece in a factory in the Kirov district. No acknowledgment was made of the Piaggio company or even Corradino D'Ascanio, the man who invented the Vespa in the first place. The Soviets didn't recognise 'capitalist' patents and trademarks, and courtesy of the Iron Curtain there was nothing Piaggio could do about it. Realising they would never get a rouble from the Russians, they instead launched a series of newspaper advertisements that gently pointed out that while the Russians used a Sputnik to travel in space, they 'relied on a Vespa to travel on the ground'.

Svetlana invited us into the villa to see the rooms and her influence was immediately apparent. There were thick, red velvet curtains and embroidered rugs thrown over the flagstone floor. The furniture was very St Petersburg – gilded and intricately carved – and there were old religious icons on most of the walls. They were family heirlooms, obviously, and I imagined Svetlana arriving in Fiesole with them all in the boot of her Trabant.

The place was fantastically quirky, more like a Transylvanian castle than bland Bella Tuscany, especially the full medieval suit of armour standing guard at the top of the stairs. The room Svetlana showed us was a little cramped but equally eccentric. At €50 a night, including breakfast, it was good value, too, so we said we'd take it.

The rain came again and fell in fat heavy drops,

slowly and deliberately, on the leaves on the trees outside our window. We were the only guests staying in the villa so it seemed very, very quiet. The thick velvet curtains soaked up any noise we made and the only sound we heard, apart from the rain, was the sound of Svetlana's young daughter playing in a far corner of the building. She played alone, chatting animatedly to herself, her voice, faint and lilting, echoing around the building in a disconcertingly disconnected way.

'Sounds a bit like a ghost, doesn't it?' said Sally. It was the kind of villa where you could quite easily convince yourself of such things.

The rain eased and we heard someone chopping wood. When I looked out of our room's tiny window I spotted a man I assumed was Svetlana's husband, Franco. He was brutish-looking, with a big head, big hair and a big moustache. He had mournful eyes, huge hands, and a barrel-shaped chest honed by lugging bales of hay.

'Looks like an axe murderer,' I said. He did have a bit of a Jack-Nicholson-in-*The-Shining* thing happening.

'Oh, great,' said Sally. 'And we're the only ones out here for miles around!'

Breakfast was served downstairs the next morning in a dining room that featured both a nineteenth-century Russian tapestry and a twentieth-century Karaoke machine. There was a basket of fresh crusty bread on the table and a selection of cheeses and salami was laid out on a silver platter that Svetlana had probably smuggled out of Russia as well. Surprisingly, it was Svetlana's husband Franco, the woodchopper, who stood behind the bar making the coffee on an old espresso machine, the levers looking tiny in his big, meaty hands. He wore an apron and had a towel slung over his shoulder, too, giving him a look that screamed Little French Maid. Well, maybe not so little, but it showed me just how wrong first impressions can be.

'Axe murderer, eh?' said Sally. 'Well, the axe murderer makes pretty good coffee.'

Svetlana seemed in better spirits, too, especially when we said we would be staying another night. Sally asked if there was a laundry she could use to do some washing, and Svetlana said to give it to her and she'd do it for us.

Tosca was not being performed until 9.15 that night so Sally and I ventured back to Fiesole and then down the hill to visit Florence.

The city gets five million visitors each year and I swear that most of them were there that day. The area around the Duomo was heaving. There were literally thousands of camcorder-toting tourists, every one of them, it seemed, with their own personal hawker intent on selling them a pair of sunglasses or at the very least a poorly reproduced copy of Botticelli's *Birth of Venus*. The Loggia del Bigallo, where abandoned children waited to be claimed by their parents in the fifteenth century, was now full of German families looking for little Hans, who they lost some time between popping into the Duomo and visiting the Baptistery.

It didn't get any better away from the cathedral. Via dei Calzaiuoli and the other tiny lanes that led towards Piazza della Signoria and the River Arno were clogged with people like the exits of a football ground after a big match. The lines outside the Uffizi were as long as the ones for toilets at half-time, and just as they would then, people shifted uncomfortably from one foot to the other. It struck me that, in Florence, culture is a spectator sport. Instead of coming to see Beckham or Ronaldo, the crowds were here to see the work of Michelangelo and Botticelli.

There was some respite at Piazza della Signoria. For centuries the piazza has been the city's big venue for public rallies and festivities, and it was the only place in Florence that offered anything even remotely like elbow room. Space here, in arguably the world's most impressive outdoor sculpture gallery, was a fluid and temporal thing. It existed only for a moment, in the precious seconds after one coach-load of tourists departed and before another arrived.

The sculptures scattered around the piazza formed a kind of three-dimensional, interactive version of *The World's Greatest Sculptures . . . Ever!* Both Cellini's bronze statue of Perseus and Giambologna's *The Rape of the Sabine Women* are tucked under the Loggia dei Lanzi. You've got the Grand Duke Cosimo I on his bronze horse in the middle of the square and Neptune and his mates ten or so metres away. And at the entrance to the old palace stands a replica of Michelangelo's *David*.

'I never realised David had such a great arse,' said Sally, admiring the 5-metre copy. 'He's got a *really* great arse.'

Foolishly I asked her what she thought of my backside.

'Yours is more like that one,' she said, pointing to the baggy-arsed statue of Neptune a few metres away.

She was joking, of course, and I know it was irrational to be jealous of David, but jealous I was. To make matters worse, I was reminded of my foolishness every way I turned. As well as the replica of David in Piazza della Signoria, there was the real one in the Galleria dell'Accademia and another replica up in the Piazza Michelangelo. Every souvenir stall and shop in Florence – and there are thousands of them – sold David postcards, alabaster statues, aprons and even underpants designed in such a way that their wearer possessed all that David had, including a fair approximation of his arse.

I was very tempted to buy a pair of the undies – you'd be hard-pressed to find a tackier souvenir anywhere else in the world, I reckon – but the look Sally gave me suggested that it would not be a good idea. In the end I bought her a book about David from the Uffizi gift shop. It featured close-up pictures of various parts of his anatomy, including his bottom. It was my way of saying sorry.

The Uffizi is set in a suite of offices built for Duke Cosimo I in 1580 and is perhaps Italy's most famous art gallery. It houses arguably the greatest collection of Renaissance art in the world and the queues to get in are equally legendary. It's not unheard of for people to wait for up to four hours, especially in summer, and in a bid to lessen the strain the gallery has introduced a pre-booking scheme. You ring up a toll-free number, nominate the date and time you want to visit and tickets are put aside for you at the door. You arrive ten minutes before your allotted time, entering through a special doorway, and then right on time you are ushered into the gallery.

I'd booked our tickets to the Uffizi the day before and was given the time I wanted without any fuss. Most visitors to Florence that day seemed to have decided to visit the museum as a bit of an afterthought and the queue to get in snaked around the Uffizi corridor and back out into the Piazza della Signoria. As Sally and I made our way to the special entrance for those with pre-booked tickets the queuing tourists clucked at us like we were queue jumpers. I felt like snatching their guidebooks out of their hands and pointing out the telephone number for the Uffizi booking office. It was in all of them.

There are 2395 pieces in the Uffizi collection and only 500 are on display at any given time. The amazing thing is that every single piece comes from one family's collection, a collection that was bequeathed to the people of Florence in 1743 by Anna Maria Ludovica of the Medicis, a family that held power in Florence almost continuously from 1434 until 1743. They were kind of like the Packer family in Australia today, but I don't expect Kerry and James to leave such a legacy to the people of Australia when they're done with the place.

Five hundred pieces of art is a hell of a lot to look at and I sympathised with the South African woman who squeezed past to the top of the queue into the room containing Michelangelo's *The Holy Family*. When someone in the queue protested she snarled that she was just trying to see if it was worth lining up for. She stormed off so it obviously wasn't.

My favourite thing about going to important art galleries like the Uffizi is to see the stuff I already know. Sally likes exploring galleries and admiring each piece of art on its own merit. I like the crowd pleasers, the paintings that are part of the world's collective subconscious, even if we haven't all seen them. In particular, I like being surprised by how different they are to how I expected.

For example, that day, I discovered that the colours of Botticelli's *The Birth of Venus* are less vibrant than they appear in reproductions. And that Titian's *The Venus of Urbino*, a favourite with pub owners the world over, is somehow lewder. I was also happy to note that *The Duke and Duchess of Urbino* by Piero della Francesca is much bigger than it appears on the cover of the Penguin classics.

After we had finished fighting our way through the Uffizi Sally and I wandered down to the river to admire the Ponte Vecchio. The crowds were even thicker there, and tourists queued up to have their photo taken beside the bridge as if it were a visiting rock star. The temperature had climbed well into the thirties and the heat and the crowds had left Sally feeling a trifle dehydrated. I tried to buy her a drink but every shop-keeper in every shop I went to was under the impression that water had recently attained the same value as gold. I wouldn't – I couldn't – hand over that much cash for something I could get by turning on a tap.

Then we stumbled upon a cheerful little sandwich shop just off the cathedral square on Via dello Studio. Drinks cost pretty much the same as they did in super-markets. And it served sandwiches that were fresh and tasty and the sort of price you'd expect to pay.

The décor was nothing to write home about – there was wood panelling on the wall and the red and white diagonally striped laminate tables were a little rough on the synapses. But the little old guy who owned it seemed eager to please. He brought the sandwich over to you personally and waited until you took your first bite to see if it was acceptable. I was flabbergasted that an establishment like this still existed in Florence.

As I paid I was tempted to take the owner aside and say, 'You do realise you're in Florence, don't you? You're barely 20 metres from the Duomo and could charge at least four times these prices and no one would bat an eyelid!' But I figured that the snack shop mafia of Florence would pay him a visit soon enough, anyway, and set him straight. And besides, if the opera ended up being cancelled because of rain, at these prices Sally and I might just pop down again for dinner.

As if on cue, the heavens opened an hour before *Tosca* was due to begin and the stage, nestled in the remains of the Roman amphitheatre, was declared too slippery and too dangerous for it to go on. Half an hour later the clouds still hung threateningly over the hills of Fiesole and the decision was made to give people a refund or to reissue tickets for another night's performance. It seemed a perfectly reasonable arrangement to me but the Italian ticket holders, many dressed in tuxedos and expensive evening wear, gesticulated at the woman in the box office as if they had just caught her crapping in their hallway.

Sally and I had eaten at a small trattoria earlier so we changed the date of our tickets to one closer to Sally's date of departure and decided to return to the villa. Over the past two days Sally had become very adept at picking up when Sophia was going to throw a hissy fit, and listened to the sound of the engine to tell when it was time to jump off. That night I jumped off, too, and walked beside the bike with Sally, using the throttle to power Sophia to a point where we could both clamber on again.

When we arrived, Svetlana and Franco were sitting at one of the outside tables drinking wine with another couple we hadn't seen before. Their daughter, Anastasia, was still up and she ran over to Sally, grabbing her hand to show her the dog that the couple had brought with them. Svetlana smiled and waved for us to join them, and while Franco was fetching another two glasses, she introduced us to the couple. Stefano owned the neighbouring farm and Natasha was his wife.

'She is from Rooo-shia, too,' said Svetlana. 'She came to Italy first. Stefano told Franco how good Rooo-shian wife is and he come look for me.'

Svetlana was the only one of them who spoke

English so she translated both their questions and our answers. Soon Franco and Stefano fell into a deep discussion about crop rotation and Natasha returned home with a headache from the wine. With Franco occupied Svetlana felt free to speak more openly with us. She told us that things were tough financially. They weren't getting as many guests as they had hoped and keeping such a big house warm, especially in winter, was fiendishly expensive. She wanted to supplement their income by getting a job, but Italian law wouldn't allow her to work.

'There is *nuthink* I can do here,' she said. 'At least in Rooo-shia I could work in a factory!'

Franco was unaware of what Svetlana was saying and if he was anything like blokes in most parts of the world, I don't think he would have been too pleased about his wife detailing their financial woes to complete strangers. He paused in his conversation with Stefano, blissful in his ignorance of what was being said, and raised his glass to us with a hearty 'Cin cin!'

We drained our glasses, said goodnight and made our way up the stone stairs to bed. As always I patted the suit of armour for luck as we passed and a sobering thought struck me. It was my last night as a 39-year-old.

CHAPTER THIRTEEN

Siena

Kinder Surprise Toy: Kitchen Pot Spy
(K02-049)

When I decided to spend my fortieth birthday riding a Vespa around Italy I imagined I would pass my big day driving through rolling hills of vineyards, the sun on my face and the smell of rural Tuscany in my nostrils. I'd lunch in a hilltop trattoria somewhere in Chianti and spend the night in a cosy inn behind the aged walls of a venerable medieval town.

Of course, what we imagine and what actually happens are often two totally different things. But I'm glad to report that my fortieth birthday passed pretty much as planned.

The day started with a typically hearty breakfast of

salami, cheese and crusty bread at the Villa Le Capanne and a hug from Svetlana when she found out it was my birthday. She gathered Anastasia and Franco on the porch of the villa for a photo before we left and then waved goodbye as we rode away.

We travelled south along the S222, better known as *Chiantigiana*, the Chianti Way, because it passes through the Chianti wine-growing region. The hills were covered with vineyards, and here and there were farm-houses, villas and baronial castles. The forest of signs at each crossroad, no matter how insignificant, suggested that most were now hotels or rental apartments. The traffic through here was heavier, too, although you'd be hard-pressed to spot a vehicle that was registered in Italy. This was by far the most popular tourist route in Italy, so most cars bore German and Dutch number-plates as well as the occasional French, Belgian or English one.

The Chianti region is one of the most popular tourist spots in Italy and for good reason. The whole stretch of road from Grassina to Castellina in Chianti looked like it had been art-directed to appear in one of those beautifully photographed Tuscan cookbooks. Each valley was ablaze with sunflowers, each ridge auto-graphed by a single line of cypress trees. Even the most modest of villas had freshly painted shutters and flower boxes overflowing with red geraniums. In the more upmarket ones old wooden carts, complete with wicker baskets, leant lazily against the walls.

We ate lunch in Castellina in Chianti in a trattoria overlooking a ridiculously picturesque valley. It was a popular spot with tourists driving through the region, and the carpark was littered with campervans, stationwagons and sedans from all over Europe. Among them was a shiny new Porsche Boxster, owned by a German chap who looked like the former Iraqi deputy prime minister, Tariq Aziz. He was wearing pastel colours inappropriate for a man of his years, which suggested he was recently divorced. His companion, an elegant blonde with teased hair, was considerably younger than he was, and she laughed uproariously at all his jokes and reached across and brushed crumbs from his moustache throughout the meal. As they drove off he floored the Boxster, causing the tyres to screech as they hit the bitumen and startling the other diners.

'Someone's got a very small penis,' Sally said between mouthfuls of pasta, and all the other female diners snickered.

I remember reading an interview with Tony Brancato, a Vespa mechanic in Leichhardt, the heart of Sydney's little Italy, who said that men who drove big, loud motorcycles were just trying to prove their manhood. 'Vespa riders,' he said, 'are content with what they have and know how to use it.' And discerning women knew that, he claimed.

Tony has been riding Vespas for close to fifty years

so it's probably safe to say that he has his own barrow to push. But there was a kernel of truth in what he said. Thanks to movies like *The Wild One*, starring Marlon Brando, a Harley Davidson was seen as the domain of the dangerous loner. But there was something refreshing, reassuring and eminently likeable about Vespas. And it wasn't a disadvantage. The girls *did* dig them. On every Vespa poster, in so many movies, you'd always see a gorgeous girl on the back. And not some troubled little vixen trying to get back at her parents by going out with a bad boy, either. She was always a well-dressed, well-adjusted beauty with brains *as well as* large breasts. At least, that's how I saw it.

Our plan was to spend the evening in the San Gimignano, the 'city of beautiful towers', and one of the best-preserved medieval towns in Tuscany. With its skyline of tall towers it has been dubbed the 'Manhattan of Tuscany', and as we approached each of the towers was bathed in the golden glow of the afternoon sun. Only fourteen towers remain of the seventy-six towers it began with in the thirteenth century – but the comparison with New York is apt.

The busloads of German and American tourists were leaving as we arrived, returning to their hotels in Florence or Siena. They were hot and cranky and loaded up with wine and olive oil that they had bought from stores playing New Age music to soothe their jangled nerves. Some stragglers were taking last-minute photos of their partners posing at one of the ancient city gates. 'Can you see my smile?' one American asked her husband through gritted teeth. 'Make sure you can see my smile!'

Before leaving London Sally had booked a room for us in the Hotel L'Antico Pozzo. It was set in a fifteenth-century townhouse on Via San Matteo, inside the city walls and only a couple of hundred metres from the Duomo square. Without question it was the most elegant hotel I had ever stayed in.

I must admit that I've never felt completely comfortable in hotels like L'Antico Pozzo. The wrought-iron furniture, the lilies in vases and the crisp, white sheets all make me feel uneasy. I always get a feeling in the pit of my stomach that I shouldn't be there or that I'm going to break something.

Having been shown to our room, I wandered about, looking at things, not quite sure what they were for, and holding them up to my face for closer inspection.

Sally caught me staring quizzically at a small linen mat beside the bed and rolled her eyes. 'It's so your feet aren't shocked by the cold of the terracotta floor tiles in the morning,' she said, exasperated. 'Want a beer?'

She made for the minibar and I felt compelled to physically restrain her. After years of travelling on a tight budget I'd disciplined myself to not even open the minibar door lest I be tempted by the tiny bottles of spirits or succumb to the siren song of a cold beer. I knew that to weaken, even for one packet of peanuts, would wreak havoc on my finances. Sally was different. As a publicist she was constantly touring with authors and was used to taking stuff from the minibar.

I drank one beer, on the pretext that it was my birthday, but couldn't say that I really enjoyed it.

I found a brochure about the history of the hotel building and read out choice snippets to Sally. The Inquisition used it in the 1600s as a venue to 'ask a few questions'. And in the eighteenth century it acquired an international reputation as a centre of 'vivacious gatherings and parties'. They were quite some parties, it seems. Girls who refused to submit to the *droit de seigneur* were suspended in the well for three days and three nights. I asked Sally if she had something similar planned for my birthday and she gave me a particularly withering stare. Obviously not, then.

It was only 4 pm when we ventured back out onto the narrow cobbled streets of San Gimignano but the last of the daytrippers were gone and we pretty much had the town to ourselves. The stores selling the Tuscan oils, wines and condiments were empty, the signs saying 'Don't Touch!' in five different languages on giant stuffed boars swinging in the breeze. Even the Collegiata Cathedral was empty. It is famous the world over for its murals painted by Taddeo di Bartolo but the television screen attached to the high-tech system that monitored and limited the number of visitors indicated that we would be the only ones inside.

Now, I don't know about you, but when I wander into a church I don't expect to be confronted by a picture of a demon defecating into a woman's mouth. Or other demons having lots of sex – unnatural sex – with a wide variety of men, women and children. But those are the scenes Taddeo di Bartolo chose to slap on the walls of the Collegiata Cathedral back in 1393. The local bishop had told him to paint something cautionary so there were frescoes of people being tortured with scorpions, buggered by demons and eating the shit of a monkey-faced goon. I suspect that if more churches had followed the lead set by Taddeo we may well have been a more God-fearing lot today.

We ate dinner at Ristorante Dorandò, a restaurant just behind the Piazza del Duomo. It specialised in Slow Food, which involves several small courses served at hourly intervals. It sounded like gastro-torture to me but Sally assured me that it was all the rage. The imposing fourteenth-century stone walls and simple yet elegant table settings were a long way from the chequered tablecloths of the Pizza Hut in Liverpool where I spent my eighteenth birthday.

The waiter presented us a menu and suggested the Slow Food tasting menu, consisting of at least twelve different dishes. I was keen to finish my meal while it was still my birthday and stuck to the à la carte menu, which contained dishes based on Etruscan, medieval and Renaissance recipes. The food was served promptly and was fantastic, although the portions were a little on the small side. The mint *pici*, a thick hand-made pasta green with mint and served with a walnut sauce, was unforgettable.

Wine was decanted with great ceremony at a table in the middle of the restaurant by a woman in a suit. Her sole task was to pour the contents of a bottle into a glass decanter, swill it around and then present it reverentially to the diners who ordered it. We had chosen one of the least expensive wines on the menu and I shifted uncomfortably in my chair at the thought of the woman going to all that trouble with our €20 bottle of red. I needn't have worried. She brought our bottle straight to the table.

We finished with a coffee made with a 1930 Faema espresso maker, and then retired to the Piazza della Cisterna to eat gelatos, sitting on the steps of the twelfth-century well. When we returned to the L'Antico Pozzo there were four Kinder Surprises waiting on our wrought-iron bed. Sally had snuck them there as we left, and she was certain there would be a green Vespa in at least one of them. There wasn't. I got two kitchen pot spies, a car and another bloody Smurf (with a water ring, in case you're wondering). I'm pleased to say that it was the only disappointing moment of my birthday.

After two days in San Gimignano eating more gelato than a forty-year-old should, we set off along the P12 for a trundle through central Tuscany that would eventually take us to Siena. Marco had described the loop through Il Castagno, Volterra and Colle di Val d'Elsa as the most beautiful road in Italy, and that day, with the warm sun on our back, it was hard to disagree.

The only discordant note were the cyclists. It wasn't the Italian wannabe racers in Lycra here, but rather groups of middle-aged couples on pre-booked Tuscan cycling holidays. We passed them in packs, red-faced and sweating, struggling to conquer the hills of Tuscany. They had come to Italy expecting a gentle cycle and generous lunches and got a more picturesque version of the Fat Club. I entered each bend that morning convinced I would come upon one of them sprawled beside the road getting CPR.

I could understand why they were doing it. Cycling offered the opportunity to savour the Tuscan countryside at a slower pace, smelling the earth and listening to the birdsong. It certainly made more sense than what the leather-clad motorcyclists were doing. They roared through Tuscany like it was a racetrack that had to be completed in record time. But cycling did involve a bit more puff.

Travelling on a Vespa, I think, was the perfect compromise. We were going at a pace slow enough to soak up the sights and smell the smells. And at the end of the day we could walk to our room without requiring assistance. We didn't get the silence the cyclists did – how silent is it hearing your heart pound, anyway? – but in a fanciful way I think the sound of Sophia's engine was in keeping with the countryside. I came to think of it as the amplified buzzing of a summer wasp.

It was better than touring in a Porsche Boxster, it would seem. We passed Tariq Aziz and his woman just the other side of Volterra. The front left tyre was flat and the blonde didn't look very impressed at all.

When I spotted the small walled town of Monteriggioni perched on a hilltop surrounded by spectacular fields of sunflowers, I thought it was the most perfect place I had ever seen. Built in 1203 to guard Siena's northern borders against invasion by Florentine armies, it was one of those outrageously picturesque places that Tuscany seems to be full of. Dante thought that the towers in Monteriggioni's 'ring-shaped citadel' looked like giants standing in a moat.

The two hotels inside the city walls were full so we stayed in a weird villa at the bottom of the hill beside the freeway. The owners had just spent a fortune on a beautiful landscaped pool after a previous guest told them that a pool was what Germans looked for in a villa. But the Germans never came and we had the villa and the pool to ourselves.

Our room felt like a room grandmothers go to die in.

It was filled with doilies and stank of mothballs. I was going to suggest that the proprietors could perhaps give it a makeover, but after their experience with the pool I figured they wouldn't be too receptive to my ideas.

Next day we set off for Siena early, stopping to take photographs in the field of sunflowers just the other side of Monteriggioni. The field sat in a picture-postcard position, with the walled city and towers positioned in the background. It was so perfect that I suspected the sunflowers had been planted there for more artistic reasons than agricultural ones, perhaps at the insistence of a postcard photographer. I finished off a couple of rolls of film there myself.

By eleven we were approaching Siena, the walled city and the striking, 120-metre-tall Torre del Mangia ahead of us at the end of a very ordinary suburban street. I was really excited about going to Siena. Back in 1983, when I was studying medieval history at Sydney University, my mum and dad went to Europe and brought me back two really cool things from Siena: a leather jacket and a painting of an Italian knight riding between two hilltop towns.

I cut a stylish swathe through my final years at university in my leather jacket before it was stolen from the student house I was living in. The thieves didn't get the painting, though. It still sits on my mantelpiece – a rectangle of old wood, gnawed by weevils, with rusty rings on the back. It's a copy of a fresco painted by Simone Martini in 1330 of the mercenary Guidoriccio da Fogliano, a southern bloke who was often called upon to help out when the Florentines made one of their frequent rampages south. The original is on a wall in the Palasso Pubblico in Siena, and I've wanted to go to Siena ever since.

Because we were riding a motor scooter we were able to enter the old city instead of having to park in one of the giant parking stations that surround the town, like other tourists. We could ride into the centre, along cobbled streets and among pedestrians, right up to the doors of hotels, where Sally would jump off and ask if there was a room available. They were all full but after an hour we were still in good spirits. My heart went out to the poor souls, hot and tired and loaded up with luggage, doing the same thing on foot.

After visiting ten or so hotels we decided to use the room-finding service offered by the Siena Hotels Promotion, situated in a kiosk near the Stadio Comunale.

When I finally got to the head of the queue the guy serving introduced himself as Alfredo. He said that he liked my scooter. 'That's mine over there,' he said, pointing to a PX. I'd parked right next to it. 'It's okay, but yours is a classic.'

As he searched his database for a room Alfredo asked me where I had bought the bike and about my travels so far. He loved the story about finding Sophia on the Internet and that I was travelling through Italy this way.

'You are the kind of tourist we want in Italy,' he said with a flourish. 'Not like these people.' He waved his arm derisively at the queue of people lined up behind me. The Japanese didn't know that they'd just been insulted and neither did the Germans. But a middle-aged English couple did and they tutted indignantly.

Alfredo found us a room in a hotel with extensive views over the valley. It was a twenty-minute walk to the Piazza del Campo, the heart of the old city, but on Sophia we could be there within minutes. We took a mid-afternoon nap and at four, just as the sun began to cast shadows on the golden stone walls, we set off on Sophia to explore.

I parked her with a clump of other Vespas beside Il Campo (the locals' affectionate name for the main square) and we set off up Via dei Pellegrini towards the Duomo. Siena's cathedral is one of the most spectacular in Italy and one of the few south of the Alps built in full spiky-columned Gothic style. It was built between 1136 and 1382, taking close to 250 years to complete. A nave on the south of the cathedral was started, the plan being to make the church the largest in Christendom. But a plague killed off most of the population and it remained unfinished. The nave now forms a kind of triumphal arch.

I love the fact that in those days people would start

building, knowing that it would take 100 years or so to complete. There was no way you were going to be around to cut the ribbon. In fact, you'd be lucky to see it get beyond the laying of foundations. You had to hope that in a couple of hundred years your successors would give you appropriate kudos in the opening speech and didn't take all the glory for themselves. And what about those successors? They had to continue with a project they'd had no say in. They could always add an extra nave or a Gothic arch, I guess. But what if they had really wanted to build a bathhouse instead?

And how did the people of Siena know that it would be the biggest cathedral in Christendom? There was nothing to stop some other city deciding to build an even bigger church a few decades later. Sure, you'd be finished first, but don't you think it would be demoralising over those final 100 years to know that the good folk of Reims were well on the way to building an even bigger cathedral. You might have the biggest church for a decade or two, but by the time the Pope heard about it, he'd be getting all excited by the next one. Having said all that, the Sienese have a church they can be mighty proud of. It's big. It's beautiful. And, unlike the Duomo in Florence, there was plenty of room just to stand back and admire it.

Inside Siena's Duomo the striking black and white striped columns reminded me of humbug lollies. Sally thought it looked like the tombs in the Valley of the

Kings. She was right. And the columns were reminiscent of the ones in Luxor. The colours used inside the cathedral were the same as the ones used on the Pharaohs' death masks.

A sermon was being held near the Chapel of Saint John the Baptist, and I was surprised that it was quite evangelical – or 'happy clappy', as Sally put it. The priest delivered it like he was in the deep south of America, and then led the congregation in singing 'Michael Rowed the Boat Ashore'. I would have played something more solemn, but I guess the Italian church is having trouble getting bums on seats too.

We ate at an *osteria* on Via dei Pellegrini called Il Ghibellino, which I chose because I liked their sign. It featured three medieval soldiers in a bowl with shields using a fork, knife and spoon respectively as their lances. Il Ghibellino turned out to be an inspired choice. It was a dark, warm, inviting place where people ate side-by-side at long wooden tables under the mournful gaze of the Sienese who populated the old black and white photos hanging on the walls. The food was excellent, especially the zucchini tarts and the roasted artichokes. The tone of the evening was set when I pointed to hairy boar on the menu and Sally said, 'Why would I want a hairy bore when I've already got one?'

After the meal we wandered back to Il Campo, the huge square that is the heart of the city. Il Campo is shell-shaped and bordered by elegant *palazzi*, and was once a field where the Council of Nine, the representatives from the different quarters of Siena, would meet to govern the medieval city. A few weeks later a bareback horse race, the Palio, would be held there and the square would be crammed with thousands of people, but that night it was peaceful and uncrowded, a gentle hum coming from the restaurants surrounding it.

Sally and I lay back on the terracotta cobblestones so we could get a 360-degree view of the floodlit buildings. A small jazz band playing in one of the restaurants behind provided the perfect soundtrack.

An old couple on their evening *passeggiata* tutted as they passed. Then a group of ferals appeared – hedge monkeys, as Sally called them – and began playing bongos near the Gaia fountain, a perfect nineteenth-century replica of the original fountain built in 1419, and featuring an array of figures, foliage, cornices, steps, pilasters and coats of arms. The bongo players were totally bereft of rhythm and their discordant thumping ruined the mood. As we left I wondered whether they had done it on purpose, driving everyone away so they could jump into the fountain and have a wash.

A few days later we headed south through an area known as the Crete. It was the Tuscany of our collective subconscious. Flame-shaped cypresses lined the fields and dirt roads wound into the hills. Ancient stone buildings crowned hilltops to catch a cool summer breeze. Olive trees, vineyards and golden fields of maize created a scene so lovely it was almost too much to comprehend. But for a good deal of it we felt like we were in the world's most attractive construction zone. Every farmhouse and every villa seemed to have a huge mechanical crane poking out of the top of it and a gang of hard-hatted workmen waiting to get to work.

It was lunchtime by the time we reached Pienza so we stopped at a small café, the only place open. It was full of people watching a live telecast of the French Grand Prix. Everyone – girls, boys, old women, even dogs – was watching the progress of Michael Schumacher. The fortunes of the Ferrari Formula One team is an obsession that transcends all barriers. The girl behind the counter was so engrossed with Schumacher's battle with Kimi Raikkonen she didn't serve us until the German had won the race. I think she deliberately gypped us with the Kinder Surprises, too. We got another couple of pot spies.

Sally was not impressed. 'Another bloody teapot!' she said as she split open the plastic container that held the toy. 'It's worse than getting a jigsaw.'

Our goal that evening was Montepulciano. At 605 metres above sea level it is one of the highest of the hill towns in Tuscany. Perched on a narrow limestone ridge it was clearly visible 20 kilometres away. When the town came into view, catching the afternoon sun like a sunbather, I decided it was time for us to look for a room for the night.

But every villa and *agriturismo* we called into was full. Most had been let out completely to Germans, who scowled at us from pools where they were invariably tossing inflated beachballs at each other. They had booked their villas months ahead – indeed, many were probably annual visitors – and they looked upon us as chancers, people who didn't have the discipline to book early.

Sally suggested that we try in the town. It was home to Tuscany's most famous red wine, the incomparable Nobile di Montepulciano, made from sangiovese grapes grown on the surrounding hills. But I wanted to have one last shot and 3 kilometres before Montepulciano I spotted it. A hand-painted sign pointing down a dirt road to Villa Maxxi, an *albergo* that also sold wine and olive oil.

Villa Maxxi was a red stone villa that was either in the process of falling apart or being reconstructed – it was hard to tell. Disrepair sat well with it, though, and the large oak wine barrels abandoned against the wall, fading and rotting, gave the place a rustic charm that many of the better-maintained villas lacked. I wandered around the outside of the building calling out '*Buona sera*', but the place seemed deserted. The attached shop, little more than a shed, really, with cases of wine and oil on the floor, was closed, but eventually I found a door with a doorbell and rang it. There was no answer.

I was about to leave when I noticed a faded piece of paper tacked to the door with a mobile phone number on it. I called the number and when a guy answered I asked in pidgin Italian whether there was a room available. The guy said something back, but my Italian wasn't up to understanding what he said. Not sure how the conversation went, I was about to hang up when a ruffled farmer opened the door, still holding his mobile phone.

If I was a betting man I would have laid money that this guy was going to tell us to go away. He looked tired and cranky and answered every question I asked with a huff. In the end he let out a sigh of resignation and said we could have a room on the solemn understanding that we only stay one night and didn't expect him to cook or clean for us.

The room was fantastic, a vast rustic space at the side of the villa with French doors framed picturesquely by a grapevine. It had an attached diningroom and kitchen, but he charged us for using it as a double room rather than an apartment. He closed and bolted the door to the kitchen and diningroom to ensure we didn't make a mess he'd have to clean up.

Our room had views across a valley to Montepulciano. A beautiful church built in honey and cream-coloured travertine, a light-coloured calcareous rock found near springs, sat at the bottom of the ridge, crowned by the town and lapped by a field in the foreground. The late afternoon sun gave it a warm glow and a flock of sheep tended by a shepherd wheeled before it. It was a perfect Tuscan scene and I wondered why we were the only people staying there. If it had had a pool I'm sure it would have been heaving with tourists. Perhaps that's why the guy had never put one in.

The church we could see from our room was the Madonna di San Biagio, and we visited it on our way into town for an evening meal. Inside, the church had been decorated extensively with fresh sunflowers. They were strung around like oversized daisy chains or placed in garlands at the small shrines. We lit a candle, not so much in hope for a good trip, but in thanks for how wonderful our journey had been already.

CHAPTER FOURTEEN

Cortona

Kinder Surprise Toy: Green Vespa
(K02-028)

There was a time back in the late 1990s when you couldn't walk past a bookstore without seeing a poster advertising books by Frances Mayes. The posters were simply enlarged versions of the books' covers, which featured captivating images of a rustic Tuscan life. On the cover of *Under the Tuscan Sun* was a stone villa set on a hill catching the cool afternoon breeze, a small chapel nearby surrounded by cypresses. *Bella Tuscany* featured the same villa but from a different angle, the cypresses clearer and taller, a sea of yellow flowers in the foreground. They were book covers that launched a thousand rash resignations. Just looking at them made you want to chuck it all in and move to Italy.

The books chronicled American Frances Mayes's trials and tribulations as she renovated a villa in Cortona, a small hilltop town in eastern Tuscany. Both books were international bestsellers and they single-handedly put Cortona on the tourist map. The town now gets visitors from as far away as Japan and South America. And Frances Mayes has been made an official citizen of the town in recognition of her contribution to the local economy.

As we approached Cortona after a long day's ride, however, Sally and I discovered there's a big difference between cover art and reality.

'Is that Cortona?' Sally asked, aghast, when the town finally came into view. 'It looks like a Yorkshire mill town!'

Cortona was grey and grimy. It sat high on a hill over-looking a flat expanse of commercial farmland a million miles from the images that inspired so many people to pack up and head off to Tuscany. We rode up a narrow winding road into town, thinking that maybe Cortona would reveal its beauty there. But it was just as dark and oppressive among the narrow, steep streets, and packs of mostly English and American tourists wandered around in a daze.

Like us the tourists tottered down Vicolo del Precipizio, or Precipice Alley, in the hope that things would get better at the bottom. They had no doubt explicitly asked their travel agent to send them where Frances Mayes lived, expecting, like me, that it would be a place of hay, herbs and sumptuous Tuscan feasts. Instead, as Sally had rather aptly put it, they got a mill town. A mill town with better ice cream, it has to be said, but a mill town, nonetheless.

Disappointments like this hit us harder. Sophia was not a powerful bike so it took us longer to cover the distances that other tourists knocked off in half a day. They could chalk down Cortona as a bad experience and get back to Florence or Perugia before the sun set. It had taken us the good part of a day to get to Cortona, passing through pretty towns like Montefollonico and Torrita di Siena that, quite frankly, would have been much nicer to stay in. But we were stuck in Cortona. And, as luck would have it, all the hotels in town were full.

The area around Cortona is thick with *agriturismi*, thrown up to cash in on the Frances Mayes phenomenon, so I knew we wouldn't be sleeping in a ditch by the side of the road that night. In fact, we found somewhere to stay fairly easily, in Villa Vaffanculo, a renovated sixteenth-century convent at Piazzano, a small village on the road to Montanare and only 6 kilometres from Cortona.

Of course, it wasn't really called Villa Vaffanculo. Or even Villa Fuck You, the literal English translation. That's just the name Sally and I christened it after the owner, Alfonso, revealed his true character in a series of petty and mean-minded incidents over the next two days. But I'm jumping ahead of myself a bit.

Villa Vaffanculo was set on a working farm and winery that produced its products organically, without chemical additives and under the strict guidelines of the Italian Association of Biological Agriculture. Well, that's what the brochure said and, to be fair, I didn't spot any bags of superphosphate hidden in dark corners of the sheds.

We were greeted on our arrival by Alfonso's son Bruno. He was a gangly, lively young guy who was more impressed that I was from Australia than with Sophia. 'I spent six months in Western Australia, learning the business,' he said enthusiastically. 'Come, you must have some wine with me!'

We sat at an outdoor table and admired the villa. It had been beautifully restored and the pool was surrounded by gardens that were elegant and simple. The wine, unfortunately, was a little less sophisticated. It was a robust red that not only removed tartar from your teeth but stripped the enamel off as well. We smiled awkwardly at Bruno as he watched us drink it, trying hard to hide the new black stains on our previously pearly whites.

'It is good, no?' asked Bruno. 'We grow it here. Your wine is okay in Australia, but you have much to learn.'

Bruno told us that he had been arrested and

interrogated on his arrival in Perth, not for crimes against dentures, but rather as a suspected terrorist. He had arrived in Australia just after the September 11 attacks in New York and immigration officers were jittery that something similar might happen in Australia. They found a map in his bag with various towns circled on it and they suspected the worst. In fact, they were wineries and when that was verified the immigration officers covered their embarrassment by fining him $110 for a few slices of mortadella he had in his bag. It must have been a terrifying experience for a nineteen-year-old bloke on his first trip abroad, but Bruno told the story with such wide-eyed enthusiasm I found myself wishing I'd been arrested as an international terrorist, too.

Our room was in the renovated barn and had been decorated by someone with a severe sunflower fetish. There were sunflower motifs on all the towels and washers, as well as on the complimentary soap and shampoos that sat in a wicker basket on the basin. The bed was covered by a sunflower-patterned bedspread and there was a sunflower painting on each of the walls. Once you got over the unsettling feeling that the sunflowers were watching you, the room was quite comfortable and homely, so we agreed to stay two nights. Bruno told us about a special dinner that night to celebrate the birthday of another guest and we agreed to attend. We were tired after the long day's ride and didn't really feel like venturing back up to Cortona to eat.

The table was set up under a pergola covered in wisteria and everyone staying at the villa attended. The guest of honour was Carolina, a Dutch girl holidaying with her family in one of the other apartments. She'd turned eighteen that day and she sat with her mum and dad at the end of the long trestle table. It was a bit like an ad for pasta sauce – everyone sitting around passing bowls of steaming pasta, drinking wine and talking animatedly.

Alfonso, Bruno's father and the villa's owner, loved being the centre of attention and moved about the table chatting to all the guests, sharing jokes with the men and flirting outrageously with the women. He had the supreme confidence of someone who thought he was pretty damn special, even though his rat-like features suggested otherwise. He was particularly attentive to the ladies, circling the table to kiss their hands. When their partners weren't looking he whispered compliments in their ears or played with their necklaces so his hand stroked their necks. Some of the woman enjoyed the flattering, but most shifted uncomfortably in their seats. When he left his hand a little too long on Sally's shoulder she simply picked it up and removed it like it was a piece of lint.

We sat next to an American couple, Andy and Catherine. Andy was a freelance journalist and photographer and sat chatting happily with everyone.

He was particularly taken by our story of riding around Italy on an old Vespa and wanted to write an article about it. 'Just like *Roman Holiday*,' he said.

On hearing that Andy was thinking of writing an article, Alfonso slithered around and said he should write an article about the villa. 'It is much more interesting than a motorbike,' he said. I think he saw Andy as his key to the lucrative American market.

We never really figured out what Catherine did. She said that it was something that kept her busy for three months of the year. The clearest thing we got from her was that she had just gone through a rather messy divorce. Even though she was with Andy she lapped up Alfonso's attention, and when it was turned elsewhere she sat getting slowly pissed on the enamel-stripping red, all the while giving a blow-by-blow account of what her therapist had said to anyone who would listen. 'I am a beautiful and desirable woman,' she said morosely. 'I've just got to accept that.'

Alfonso had set up a display of firecrackers to spell out Carolina's name, and after dinner had finished he attempted to light it. It wouldn't catch fire at first and when it finally did, the 'o' didn't work properly. Alfonso's efforts were appreciated, though, and he got a kiss on the cheek from Carolina anyway. Perhaps the kiss excited him a little because he immediately put on some music and slow-danced suggestively with any woman who'd agree to dance with him.

Sally refused – I think she was concerned where his hand might end up this time. But Catherine jumped at the chance, staggering from her chair and collapsing into Alfonso's arms. Despite looking like Sean Penn in *Casino*, Alfonso thought he was Patrick Swayze circa *Dirty Dancing* and Catherine was his compliant Jennifer Grey. He put on quite a show, executing all of Patrick's best moves as well as an imitation of a full body search at airport security with him playing the guard and Catherine the canny smuggler. Neither Sally nor I could remember that one from the movie.

The next morning, just after ten, Andy knocked at our door, keen to take some photos of Sophia for the article he was planning to write. I wheeled Sophia onto the cobbled forecourt in front of the villa, positioning her so she caught the morning light. Andy took photos from all kinds of angles, changing lenses and standing on a chair to get an overview shot.

Alfonso came out of his office to see what was happening.

'Just look at this bike,' Andy said to Alfonso between shots. 'Isn't she beautiful?'

Alfonso hurrumphed and pointed out her blemishes. The flecks of rust on her running board. The flaking chrome on the bumper bar.

'That's part of her charm,' Andy enthused. 'A restored bike would be just too much.'

Alfonso suggested again that Andy write an article about the villa. When Andy ignored him, he said that he'd just been on the phone to the producers of the movie version of *Under the Tuscan Sun*.

'They might be filming a balcony scene here,' he said to Andy, trying to get his attention. 'George Clooney is coming to check it out.'

Andy said 'That's great!' but continued taking photos.

Alfonso kicked the ground and walked off. Ridiculous as it seems, it appeared he was actually jealous of Sophia – a forty-year-old lump of machinery, for Christ's sake! Worse, the look he shot me as he skulked away suggested that he blamed me personally for distracting Andy from the task at hand. That is, writing a flattering article about the Villa Vaffanculo that would have the American guests streaming in.

Andy was either unaware of Alfonso's tantrum or was ignoring it, and after he'd finished taking photos he suggested going into Cortona for lunch. He knew a great place at the back of the town that overlooked the plains below. And afterwards he would point out where Frances Mayes lived, the famous Bramasole Villa. It sounded like a plan so I went to find Sally.

Catherine wanted to ride on the Vespa so Sally travelled in the car with Andy. As we left Alfonso stood at the door and shot me a withering glance. I was definitely not in his good books.

When we reached the restaurant Sally pulled me aside and asked if I had been going slow for Catherine's sake.

I told her I was going the same speed I always did.

She laughed. 'You were crawling along!' she said and grinned. 'It was like we were going in slow motion in the car!'

Now that Sally mentioned it, Cortona *had* appeared on the horizon and then stayed there for an awfully long time. I'd had time to contemplate the church at the bottom of the hill and peer into the manicured gardens of some of the villas nearby. But with the wind in my face and the sound of the tiny two-stroke engine straining to reach speed it *felt* like I was belting along. I guess I'd adjusted to Sophia's pace.

Andy picked a table out in the sun beside a lavender hedge. The waiter came and Andy ordered without looking at the menu. He was writing an article on the restaurant, too, and knew what was good to eat. Catherine ordered *prosecco*, a sparkling Italian wine, and we sat in the warm afternoon sun getting a little drunk, the air thick with the smell of lavender.

I liked Andy. He was a typical freelancer, always looking for the next angle, but he wasn't malicious or a user. He worked hard chasing every half-lead and didn't knock back any contra that came his way. I suspected that he was getting a room out at Villa Vaffanculo on the promise of a flattering article, but hey, good luck to him. He was travelling in Italy, staying in villas, eating well and paying as little as humanly possible. It was a life many would envy.

Catherine, on the other hand, wasn't sure what she wanted to do. She was cashed up after her recent divorce, and without a house and a husband she was looking for something to focus on. 'Alfonso took me out to the villa he is renovating,' she said over lunch. 'It's only $50,000 to buy a share. He rents it out for you when he's not using it. I don't think that's too bad.'

I didn't say anything, but I found it interesting that Alfonso hadn't mentioned his Tuscan time-share opportunity to us. Nor had he talked to Andy about it. I suspect he'd sensed Catherine was ready for a Frances Mayes–style life change and he was determined to be the one to benefit.

After the meal we followed Andy and Catherine in their car down to Frances Mayes's house. Frances wasn't in – the rumour was that she was fulfilling a lifetime ambition to visit Greece – so I parked Sophia at the front gate and got Sally to take a photo with my digital camera. Frances and I are published by the same company in the UK and I wanted to send the photo to my editor to wind him up.

I'd asked my editor for the address of Frances Mayes's house before I left, not because I wanted to meet her, but rather because I was interested in seeing the house that had created so much wealth for so many

Italian real-estate agents. He'd muttered something about getting back to me, but he never did. It was worth more than his job to give out Frances Mayes's address willy-nilly. Of course, once you get to Cortona the whereabouts of the Mayes villa is an open secret, but he wasn't to know that.

I choreographed the photo so that it looked like I was calling up to someone in the house and when I sent the picture to my editor from an Internet café later that afternoon I intimated that it was Frances I was chatting to. I told him that she wouldn't let me in, despite the fact that I had mentioned his name – a number of times. Instead, I said, she asked me to spell out his name then told me to go away.

I got an email back almost immediately. 'You rotter, Mr Moore,' he wrote. He'd obviously shown the picture to someone in the company who knew what Frances Mayes's villa looked like and was hoping I was pulling his leg. But he couldn't be sure.

Over lunch Andy had mentioned that Alfonso was expecting us to eat dinner at the villa that evening so when we returned for our afternoon nap I sought out Alfonso to tell him that we were eating up at Cortona instead.

He was in his office and still smarting from Sophia stealing his limelight, it seems. 'You agreed to half-board,' he snapped. 'You can go into Cortona if you want but you will be still charged for the meal.'

We hadn't agreed to half-board. We ate at the villa the night before because it was a special occasion for the Dutch girl's birthday. I tried telling that to Alfonso but he simply waved me away with a condescending flick of his hand and went back to his paperwork. I probably should have confronted him then but I took out my frustration on the inflatable crocodile in the pool, instead. Sally thought I was doing a Steve Irwin impersonation, but I was actually pretending it was Alfonso.

That night only six people ate at the villa. Sally and I. Andy and Catherine. And an old American couple from Montana that Andy had found in Cortona. They were unhappy with the place they were staying in up in the town. They'd booked a package expecting the full Frances Mayes experience and had got a grim hotel room in the mill town instead. Andy told them they should check out Villa Vaffanculo. Andy was hustling up business for Alfonso and if everything went well the couple from Montana would move down here.

That meal was meant to be Alfonso's opportunity to dazzle and charm the couple from the mid-west. But they were a sincere, evangelical pair and Alfonso's show of slimy innuendo and Patrick Swayze-style dance moves were lost on them. When he rested his hand on the wife's neck she let out a startled yelp as if she'd received an electric shock. And on hearing one of Alfonso's ribald jokes the husband said he didn't think that sort of humour was appropriate at the dinner table. Alfonso skulked back to the kitchen, hoping a delicious home-cooked meal would save the evening.

While he was there, shouting at his daughter Claudia to add more herbs, it came up in the conversation that I had visited Iran. The couple from Montana were interested – I think they suspected there would be lots of souls to be saved in a country that was part of the axis of evil – and they asked me to tell them all about it. When Alfonso came with the food, ready to make amends for his previous faux pas, I was in the middle of a story about being kidnapped by wrestlers at a mosque. The couple from Montana told Alfonso just to plonk it down and they continued to ask me more questions.

I could see that Alfonso was getting upset, and to be honest I played it up a little, taking my time to answer the questions and expanding on my stories more than I normally would have. Alfonso retaliated by 'accidentally' bumping me when he put my plate down. It got very juvenile, and judging by the look on Alfonso's face it could easily have escalated into something more. Sally must have sensed the risk of violence and suggested we make our excuses to leave before dessert was served. Alfonso was wielding a cake-cutting knife that looked particularly large and sharp.

We rode back up into Cortona to get a gelato and sat on the steps of the Palazzo Comunale to eat it.

'Did you see Alfonso's face?' said Sally laughing. 'You really pissed him off!'

I hadn't meant to. Well, okay, maybe a little. But if he hadn't insisted on us having dinner at the villa he would have had Mr and Mrs Montana to himself. It was a rod he had created for his own back.

Still, the evening ended on a high note. After finishing our gelati we bought two Kinder Surprises. Sally's had the elusive green Vespa in it. I was so happy I almost forgot about Alfonso altogether.

Alfonso hadn't, though, and the next morning he burst into our room at 7 am, apologising that he'd thought it was Andy and Catherine's. And when we checked out I noticed that he'd charged us for the 'complimentary' wine we were served on our arrival (and Alfonso clearly felt that his rough red was worth as much as a bottle of Penfold's Grange). Worse, he'd charged me €20 for using his Internet connection for a couple of minutes.

He didn't present us with the bill personally – he was in town 'attending to business', apparently – so I was able to convince his daughter Claudia to drop the price to €5. It was still five times the price it should have been, but I considered it a minor victory nonetheless.

As we rode away from the Villa Vaffanculo I decided to put our stay there down to experience. Alfonso was typical of a certain style of Italian. He was super-nice to you as long as you had something he wanted: repeat business; cash for a time-share in his villa complex; a flattering article; a shag. But if he couldn't sell you that dream he'd make sure he 'benefited' some other way. His antics only made me appreciate all the other Italians I'd met on my trip so far. They'd helped me not for what I could give them or how much money they could screw out of me, but rather because they wanted to. Alfonso, thankfully, was an aberration.

So if you ever find yourself in Cortona, looking for somewhere to stay, can I recommend giving Villa Vaffanculo a miss? Unless you're the kind of person who enjoys having their girlfriend or wife or wallet felt up by a sleazy, short-sighted Italian guy with rat-like features, of course.

Note: The movie *Under the Tuscan Sun* premiered in the US in September 2003. Diane Lane plays Frances Mayes and Raoul Bova plays her love interest, Marcello. George Clooney is nowhere to be seen. Nor is Alfonso's balcony.

CHAPTER FIFTEEN

Massa Marittima

Kinder Surprise Toy: Bear with a Beehive
(K02-076)

My last few days with Sally passed like a slide show of
snatched moments. A night in Poppi in a hotel attached
to a castle overlooking terracotta roofs and a sea of
clotheslines. The opera in Fiesole mercifully cut short in
the second act by a sudden thunderstorm. A night
in Bagni di Lucca, an eighteenth-century spa town, in the
hills of the Garfagnana, where the rushing river kept us
awake all night. But unlike a slide show it was over before
we knew it and it was time for Sally to go home.

Poppi was a revelation. It was a tiny medieval town
that sat on a hill overlooking the Casentino Valley,
crowned by a castle that could be seen as far away as

Bibbiena. The old town was reached by a steep road lined on both sides with ancient oak trees that formed a leafy canopy. The main street, only half a kilometre long, was lined with arched arcades on either side. Tourists were still an oddity here. Little old ladies dressed from head to toe in black stopped and watched us pass.

Poppi was also the site of what came to be known as our 'Kinder Surprise Miracle'. Sadly, we were still buying them, even after finally getting the elusive green Vespa. It had become something of an after-meal ritual for us. A lot of people who come to Italy like to finish their evening with a gelato from a local gelateria. We liked to finish ours with a gelato *and* a Kinder Surprise.

Sally had developed a taste for the Kinder Surprise Merendero. The Merendero is egg-shaped, too, but instead of being an egg of chocolate wrapped in foil, it is an egg made of plastic. It separates into two halves, both sealed with a sheet of plastic. Under one is a chocolate paste not unlike Nutella, a crunchy wafer ball and a small plastic spoon to eat it with. The other half contains the toy. It is a 'summer' Kinder Surprise, apparently, brought out for those hotter months when the usual Kinder Surprise egg gets a little soggy.

Being more of a traditionalist I stuck with the original-style Kinder Surprise eggs, so each evening we'd buy one of each. That night in Poppi we both got the same toy, a bear with a beehive, from two different styles of eggs. It could have been a coincidence, but I was convinced a greater force was at work. My Kinder Surprise was a winter one, released in the early part of the year. Sally's was a summer one, appearing like a swallow for the short three months of summer. It was obvious, wasn't it? Getting the exact same bear toy from two different kinds of Kinder Surprise signified that Sally and I were meant to be together. You can't argue with stuff like that.

Our last evening together in Italy was spent in Lucca. Of all the places I had visited on my own it was perhaps my favourite. I loved the city walls that doubled as a city park and the ordered streets that locals cycled along, waving to each other. I loved the piazzas and the gelaterias and the tower with the tree on top. And I knew Sally would, too.

On the last day of my previous visit to Lucca I had discovered a fantastic bed and breakfast as I wandered down Via Sant'Andrea towards the Torre dei Guinigi. It was called La Romea and I'd noticed its battered hand-painted sign quite by chance. It was nothing extraordinary to look at from the outside but inside it was a stylish boutique hotel, and when the owners showed me around I noticed that each room was taste-fully decorated and themed in a particular colour. I booked the Red Room for Sally's last evening in Italy.

I had made a point of memorising the best way to

the hotel. I entered the walled part of the city at Porta Elisa and then turned right at Via del Fosso, following the canal where swallows love to dive bomb for insects. At Via della Fratta I hung a left at the roundabout around a statue of the Madonna to Piazza San Pietro Somaldi. A quick left, left, right and I was on Via Sant'Andrea, right near the Guinigi Tower.

The plan was to impress Sally with my intimate knowledge of Lucca, and it worked. When we arrived I rode right up to La Romea without making a wrong turn, parking Sophia in front of an arched stone doorway opposite for added effect.

The hotel was on the second floor of an old fourteenth-century palace and was run by a stylish young couple called Giulio and Gaia.

When we reached the top of the stone staircase Giulio greeted me like an old friend. 'Ahh, the Vespa rider!' he said with a grin. 'How has your journey been?'

I told him that it had been amazing and that Sophia, on the whole, had behaved herself. When I had booked the room back in June he had expressed concern about me travelling so far on such an old bike. Now he beamed a proud smile at Sophia's achievements as if she was his own child.

When Sally saw our room she let out a little yelp of delight. 'This is absolutely gorgeous!' she said, throwing open the windows and taking in the view up Via Sant'Andrea towards Via Fillungo. 'It's like something out of *Hip Hotels*!'

It's sad to admit it, but being able to walk around Lucca with Sally that afternoon and point out things knowledgeably gave me an inordinate amount of pleasure. I showed her the ring of medieval buildings that formed the Piazza Anfiteatro and explained how the empty arena shape of the square was created when the stone of the old Roman amphitheatre in the middle was stolen. I took her inside San Frediano and showed her the baptismal font as big as a fountain. And we strolled around the ramparts under the trees in the dappled afternoon sunlight. It was if I'd been born there. When Sally said that I seemed to know an awful lot about Lucca I beamed with pride. My overly long stay there the first time around, it seemed, hadn't been for nothing.

We walked down the Via Fillungo and the tour took a more personal turn. I showed her the hairdressing salon that had inflicted the Lucca Fringe on me. And I pointed out the Michael Hutchence jeans, still in the window.

When I suggested I try them on she pursed her lips and shook her head vigorously. We finished our afternoon tour eating gelato out the front of the San Martino cathedral. A wedding had just finished and Sally expressed both dismay and admiration that almost all of the women guests were wearing wide-weave fishnet stockings and ankle boots.

In the evening we ate in a tiny restaurant at a table in an alley, pretending Sally's holiday wasn't about to end, and we retired to the Red Room for our last night together.

The next morning I drove Sally to Pisa airport, parking right beside the entrance door. When she disappeared through passport control, I felt like I had lost a limb and I wandered through the terminal sad-eyed and lonely until a security guard was dispatched to send me on my way.

I was tempted to abandon Sophia and catch the next flight to London – it wouldn't be the same without Sally's hands resting on my knees – but I decided to go to Livorno and see Marco instead. I'd simply pop in like everyone else and watch him work. Or play the pinball machine. Or grab a beer. He wouldn't mind.

Marco looked up from the bike he was working on and greeted me with a big grin and a hearty '*Ciao*!' He'd finished the 1972 Super Sports and had moved on to a Spanish Primavera. (Spanish Primaveras have a different headlight apparently. Go figure!) I told him I had just put Sally on her plane.

He gave me a sympathetic shrug. 'There is a Martini

party at the local bar tonight,' he said. 'Why don't you come along?'

The bar was called Vizi e Virtù, Vices and Virtues, and it was *the* new hotspot in Livorno. It was only a block from Marco's workshop and for the evening Martini had commandeered it to launch a campaign aimed at winning back sophisticated twenty-somethings to the cause. The drink of choice for James Bond and Dean Martin, first made in Italy back in 1865, was losing out to Bacardi Breezers and Lemon Ruskis, and Martini were fighting a rearguard action, enlisting Gwyneth Paltrow as their spokesperson. Gwyneth wasn't in attendance that night but her countenance beamed enigmatically from every wall. Instead we were treated to a gaggle of Martini girls, dark-haired and dark-eyed like Audrey Hepburn, and wearing identical black and white dresses cut in a style Audrey might have worn in the 1960s.

The crowd was cooler than cool and looked like they had just come from a GQ fashion shoot. We didn't. Marco, usually a stylish man, had chosen to wear a Vespa mechanic's jacket. I was in my cords and denim jacket. And Filippo, although he had the requisite goatee, had come straight from uni in a T-shirt and jeans. We probably attacked the complimentary food a little too eagerly – it *was* sensational – and didn't do ourselves any favours by asking the Martini girls if the drinks were free. They weren't. The freebies, it seemed, were going to the cool folk.

'There is a league here,' said Filippo looking around, shaking his head. 'And we're not in it.'

The cool folk didn't look like they were having much fun, though. They slouched on stools at high tables scowling at each other, afraid that a smile might destroy their carefully cultivated image of detachment. It was the sort of situation you could imagine Dean Martin sauntering into in a tux, a highball in one hand and a cigarette in the other. He'd make a beeline for the Martini girls and effortlessly chat up not just one, but all of them. 'What are you girls doing with these chumps?' he'd say. 'Why don't you let Dino show you ladies a good time?'

I would have thought that was exactly the spirit Martini would be trying to capture by holding this soirée. Set the mood by putting on a bit of Dino and reminding these wannabes that, unlike a Bacardi Breezer, their drink had real class. Instead, some bright spark decided the music needed to be contemporary and so we were listening to the new album by the Red Hot Chilli Peppers.

The most attractive of the Martini girls liked it. When the song 'By the Way' came on she swayed to the music, then flicked her hips, and finally waved her hands in the air. If you've ever seen the Seinfeld episode in which Elaine dances, this girl was worse. In her mind I think she was dancing like a go-go dancer in a cage. But to everyone else it looked like she was having an epileptic fit.

'Such a beautiful girl,' sighed Marco. 'But such an ugly dancer!'

This was exactly the situation I'd been hoping to find myself in while I was in Italy. A sophisticated party with exotic cocktails and fantastic food and attended by elegantly beautiful women. Yet it was all wrong. Red Hot Chilli Peppers, for God's sake? I like the Red Hot Chilli Peppers but not as the soundtrack for an Italian cocktail party.

Ernest Hemingway once said that drinking Martinis made him feel civilised. It made me feel mischievous. After I had a few Martinis under my belt I went up to the bar and asked if they had any Dean Martin to play. The barman gave me a blank look so I started singing 'Volare' to try and give him a clue.

'Volare,' I moaned, swaying slightly. 'Woah, woah, woah, woah!' Let's just say I sang 'Volare' as well as the Martini girl danced.

When that didn't ring any bells I tried 'That's Amore'. The cool crowd began to be alarmed and looked at Marco and Filippo for an explanation for my strange behaviour. Marco shrugged his shoulders and said '*Australiano*' and they nodded and went back to their drinks.

I was not so easily beaten. I had another Martini and tried to get the Martini girls to do the backing vocals for 'That's Amore', or at least the ring-a-ding-a-ding part. They moved away from me with fear in their eyes so I ended up doing the backing vocals myself. I don't remember much more of the evening after that. Except that I woke up in the middle of the night on the floor of Marco's workshop.

The next day I was nursing a considerable hangover so Marco took me to a café on the beach nearby for lunch. The palm trees gave the beach a faux Riviera feel and the bright midday sun that bounced off the chrome tables gave me all kinds of grief.

Marco bought me a Kinder Surprise – it was another teapot creature – and asked me if I could do him a favour. 'I need something delivered to a friend of mine in Massa Marittima,' he said. 'His name is Federico and he runs the Pub dei Fantasmi down there. You could do it on your way to Rome.' He placed a brown paperbag on the table and pushed it towards me. It crossed my mind for a second that it might have contained drugs. The whole scene had a certain Tarantino feel about it. I opened the bag and looked inside and saw that it was a set of points.

Marco smiled when he saw the look on my face. I think it tickled his fancy that after all the trouble I'd had with Sophia's points I was bringing relief to another Vespa owner suffering the same problem. I could also see what he was doing and appreciated it. He didn't need me to be his parts mule. He could have just as easily posted the points to his friend. But he could see that I was at a loss since Sally left and that my dream of riding to Rome was floundering. By sending me off to Massa Marittima, in the far south of Tuscany, he was simply kickstarting things again.

I put the package in my bag and set off immediately, following the road south along the coast. Young Livornese were clambering down the cliffs to the pebbly beaches, where they sunbaked or swam out to the rocks just offshore.

Soon I was travelling through flat fields, the coast a kilometre or so away. The road was lined with oleander, flowering red, white and pink. Earlier in the trip I'd told Sally how my mother had impressed upon us as children how poisonous the plant was. Sally had thought it was hilarious that I still regarded oleander as 'deadly'. No doubt if she'd been here she would have made some smart crack about it being the 'most dangerous road in Italy'.

At Piombino, an ugly town dominated by iron and steel works, I turned inland towards Massa Marittima. It was a different kind of Tuscany here, hotter, drier, and the hills were covered in *macchia*, Mediterranean scrub not unlike heather. Whereas cypresses were used to mark boundaries in other parts of the region, farmers here used prickly pear cactus. Agriculture seemed more homely here, too. Farmers still produced oil, fruit and wine, but they sold it from tables set beside the road.

Massa Marittima sits high in the Colline Metallifere, with commanding views of the bleak countryside that surrounds it. The metal-bearing hills provided the town with much of its wealth during the twelfth century. The cathedral, the Palazzo Comunale and all the other impressive buildings on Piazza Garibaldi were all financed by the lead, copper and silver ore mined in the region.

Sophia attacked the long, steep road leading up to it with a gusto that was unknown when Sally was on the back.

I found the Pub dei Fantasmi, Federico's Ghost Pub, at the bottom of an alley that ran off the main square, but a sign beside the door indicated it wouldn't open until 9 pm. That was still five hours away so I set off to find a room for the night.

Kodak was sponsoring a photographic conference in Massa Marittima that week and the streets were full of photographers in vests with lots of special pockets, presumably to hold rolls of film, lenses and other paraphernalia. They obviously thought they looked like men of action, ready to head off to war to take pictures, but the effect was somewhat diminished when they stopped to have a gelato. They had also taken all the good rooms.

I found a bed in Ostelloe Clarisse, a privately run hostel in an old monastery at the top of the town. The manager had turned over the walls of the hostel to a local photographer named Roberto Franceschinis to use as an exhibition space. As they like to say in *The Sun*,

Roberto was a 'glamour' photographer and every time I left my room I was confronted by a photo of one of his naked female subjects doing something fruity.

One girl squatted in a shower. Another stood on a staircase scratching, shall we say, a very particular kind of itch. My favourite was the one of two very attractive lasses, naked as the day they were born, leaning against a bus stop chatting as if it was something they did every morning waiting for the 302 to Siena.

When I came back downstairs from my room I realised that the girl sitting at reception was one of them. 'You can sign the comments book,' she said when she caught me doing a double take. I wrote that I found the exhibition 'confrontational'. Mister Franceschinis could take that any way he chose.

I spent the afternoon on the hostel's couch reading and soaking up the sun that streamed through the window. Just on five, Miss Nude Bus Stop 2003 moved from behind the reception desk and into the lounge room to practise a spoken-word piece with a fat, grey-haired, frizzy-bearded chap playing a cello. I tried to keep reading but after sitting through the first few discordant notes I decided it was as good a time as any to go for a ride.

A small compact garbage truck was parked beside Sophia and the garbo, a guy with shoulder-length, greying hair and aviator glasses, was checking her out. He started talking to me in Italian – the Milan plates got them every time – but when I said I was from Australia he spoke to me in English. His name was Maurizo and when he spoke English every syllable was pronounced.

'She is *bea-u-ti-ful!*' he said, standing back and admiring Sophia. 'She is *un-touch-ed.*'

In my travels I had noticed that the thing Italians seemed to like best about Sophia was that she looked her age. She had not been tarted up with a poorly executed paint job but had been allowed to grow old gracefully. He asked how much I paid for her and when I told him he said it was a good price.

'You could pay €2000 for this,' he said. Old bikes like Sophia were getting rarer and rarer, he said. And, like Marco and Filippo, Maurizo blamed the government's *rotamazione* policy. 'The *bastardos* are *de-stroying* these *bea-u-ties* to sell new bikes!' he spat.

Maurizo circled Sophia again, marvelling at all her accessories, particularly the hubcaps with the card symbols. To look at him, you'd swear he was the kind of guy who would restore old V8s. He was skinny, wore tight black jeans and his hair, well, not to put too fine a point on it, the guy had a mullet. Blokes like him back home hated Vespas. But he loved them.

He asked if he could sit on Sophia, and I nodded.

'I have a 1974 Rally,' he told me proudly, as he gripped the handlebar and swivelled it from side to side. 'Sixty thousand kilometres and I have never had my hand in the engine!'

He was impressed that I had ridden from Milan. 'She is still very strong,' he said.

I told him about the problems I had had and he gave a derisive snort. It was nothing, he said, and he wrote some useful words in my notepad should they happen again. *Non scintilla* – no spark. *Scoppia* – it blasts (backfires). *Puntini* – points.

Finally, reluctantly, he announced he had to leave. He had a garbage run to finish. 'Tuscany is perfect for the Vespa,' he sighed. 'I wish I could ride with you.'

He insisted on writing his name and phone number in my notepad, just in case I came back to Massa Marittima one day. He also wrote me a message in English. 'When I saw your Vespa,' it read, 'I had *stupefatto*!' (amazement).

As he drove off he wound down his window and called out to me. 'If you need parts in Australia,' he yelled, 'give me a call!'

It was still too early to go to the Pub dei Fantasmi and deliver Marco's package, so I sat on some stone steps beside the hostel and watched the sun set across the valley. A warm breeze blew, bringing with it the aroma of cypresses. My grandmother had two cypresses growing in her front yard and I was reminded of how I played among them as a child. They had ball-like nuts, segregated in a pattern like the stitching on a soccer ball, and I'd pick them to throw at my sisters. The sticky sap would get on my hands and the smell would linger for hours.

I got a funny nostalgic feeling that made me get out my mobile and ring Sally. She was cold and miserable at work and didn't seem to appreciate my description of rolling Tuscan hills and caressing warm breezes laden with the perfume of cypress pines.

I ate in one of the restaurants on Piazza Garibaldi before retiring to the steps of the Duomo to eat a gelato. Families were taking their evening *passeggiata*. They were locals, mainly, but there were a few German and Dutch families who had ventured in from surrounding villas. A pack of fighter jets screamed low overhead and I texted Sally again. 'Are the US bombing the crap out of Iraq?'

She texted back and said it was probably just a NATO exercise.

By nine-thirty I had finished my gelato and wandered down Via Butigni to the Pub dei Fantasmi. Inside it was dark and atmospheric. Apparently jazz bands played there every night of the week.

A girl was serving behind the bar and I asked for Federico. There was a 1954 Vespa parked out the front, one of Marco's restorations, I could tell, so I knew he was in.

Marco had given me a potted history of Federico over lunch in Livorno. He was the youngest of eight brothers and once raced Vespas professionally. Then he had had an accident and his skull was fractured. He spent six months in a coma and when he woke up he walked straight out of hospital. He was missing for another three months until his brothers found him living under a bridge in Turin, with only a dog to keep him warm. That had been three years before. Now he ran a bar in the south of Tuscany.

Federico introduced himself cautiously, still not sure why there was an Australian in his bar asking for him by name. He had a shock of black hair that looked like he had stuck his finger in a power point.

When I told him Marco had sent me and gave him the brown bag with the points in it, he put his arm around my shoulder and laughed. 'Ahhhh Marco!' he grinned. '*Bastardo!*'

I filled him in on my story and his eyes lit up in astonishment. He told me I was crazy, which I thought was a bit rich from a guy who used to hurtle souped-up Vespas around racetracks. He said something to the girl behind the bar and then beckoned for me to follow. We went down some old stone steps to the cellar. He flicked the light on and there, among the cases of wine and beers, were two more Vespas, a 1960 180 SS and an early PX 125. He had parts for both bikes hidden among Super Tuscans and Brunellos, including another 180 SS in pieces.

'I love Vespas!' he said with a grin.

We went back to the bar and Federico plied me with free drinks for the rest of the evening. He insisted I stay. The band that night was Art Blakely and the Jazz

Messengers, who the poster said would feature Wynton Marsalis in 'a soulful mood'. Wynton was a jazz legend from America and looked like a puffier-faced version of Will Smith. He played the trumpet like an angel was indeed in a soulful mood.

I was, too, especially when I got a text message from Sally between sets saying that she wished she was back in Italy with me. Somehow the trip didn't feel quite the same without her.

CHAPTER SIXTEEN

Pitigliano

Kinder Surprise Toy: Smurf with Fishing Gear
(K02-066)

The Vespa 125 that made its debut in 1948 was the first new model developed after the release of the original Vespa 98 in 1946. It was the result of two years of testing and feedback and featured several important improvements. It had a bigger engine, the suspension was better and the silencer had been replaced with a much more efficient one. The saddle was sprung at the front for greater comfort and the headlight was bigger and stronger. But the most significant improvement, I think, was the bag-holder hook they added under the seat.

The hook was a simple but brilliant idea. The one-piece, pressed-steel body of the Vespa is best known for its distinctive protective leg shields and for the fact that the engine had been moved to the back of the bike. But it also created a gap between the front shield and the seat that was perfect for carrying stuff. Furthermore, the drop from the seat to the running board was exactly the right height for hanging a shopping bag. When Enrico Piaggio saw the prototype of the hook he wondered out loud why they hadn't thought of it sooner. It's a feature you'll still see on the Vespas produced today, but it's more likely to be used to carry a Thai takeaway than the weekly shopping.

The bag-holder hook had certainly transformed the nature of my trip. I bought provisions every morning as I left a town, hung the bags from the hook and then stopped for a picnic lunch somewhere suitably picturesque. Thanks to that simple metal hook under my seat I was able to eat wherever I wanted, more often than not beside a ruined abbey in the middle of nowhere, without another human being, let alone a sandwich shop, in sight.

Buying those provisions became an integral part of my journey, too. The morning I left Massa Marittima I visited the Casa della Frutta, the House of Fruit, and the woman serving gave me an impromptu Italian lesson by slowly pronouncing the name of each item as she put it on the scale. At Panificio Romano the baker suggested the *panine frusti Genovesi*, a Genovese-style bread that he sold by weight at €3.62 a kilo. At Il Salumeria, I dodged

the different-coloured and -shaped pastas in clear cello-
phane packets tied with ribbon hanging from the door,
and picked up some bocconcini, olives and local wild-
boar ham. It would have been quicker and more
convenient to visit the co-op supermarket on the outskirts of town but it wouldn't have been half as much
fun.

I finished my shopping trip with a cappuccino (it
was before 10 am so I could drink it without causing
offence) and a *bombolone* at a café on Piazza Garibaldi.
I added lots of sugar to the coffee to match the sweetness of the custard-filled doughnut, and watched a black
hearse pull into the square and stop outside the
cathedral. The church bells tolled three sad notes – up,
up, down – and everyone in town stopped and stood
still in silent respect as the coffin was carried into
the church. A couple of nuns in black hung outside,
looking like ravens, ready to comfort the mourners.
They spotted a group of old women sobbing and
swooped in, holding their hands and kissing their wet
cheeks. It seemed to help.

I headed south from Massa Marittima through an area
known as the Maremma. The ancient Romans were the

first to cultivate the marshes here. They drained the swamps and created richly fertile farming land. When the Roman Empire collapsed, however, the drainage channels became clogged and the swamps returned, transforming the entire region into a wilderness of stagnant, mosquito-infested ponds. In *The Divine Comedy* Dante compared it to the area in hell reserved for suicides – a place where leaves were not green but black, branches not smooth but twisted, and trees bore no fruit. The wild boars, however, loved it.

In the late eighteenth century Leopold II reclaimed the land, unblocking the irrigation canals and ridding the area of the malarial mosquitoes that infested it. The area became the domain of the *butteri*, Italian cowboys with a penchant for black felt hats, grey waistcoats and moustaches not unlike the one Val Kilmer wore as Doc Holliday in *Tombstone*.

The *butteri* are exceptional cattlemen. Legend has it that the only time Buffalo Bill was ever defeated in a rodeo was when he came to Italy and faced the *butteri*. Of course, Bill's people cried foul – apparently some of the exotic local lasses were sent around before the contest to distract him. But the fact remains: in a rodeo ring, deep in the heart of the Tuscan Maremma, Buffalo Bill, the most famous cowboy in the world, was laid low by an Italian with a silly moustache.

These days farming long-horned cattle in the Maremma is not the lucrative pursuit it once was. Much of the vast grazing land has been turned over to vine-yards, the homesteads turned into villas for holidaying Germans. But as I rode through I kept my eye on the low ridge in the distance, just in case I spotted a lone man on a horse, surveying this wild patch of Italy.

Not many tourists visit this part of Tuscany. For most of the morning I had the road pretty much to myself, only occasionally passing a car with Dutch or German numberplates, its inhabitants looking bewildered because they thought they were on the road to Florence. But when I reached the hot springs at Terme di Saturnia at lunchtime the road was thick with them again.

I had nicknamed these tourist vehicles 'Tuscan Taragos', after the most popular people-mover back home, the Toyota Tarago. They were the transport of choice for European families venturing out from their homes to see the wonders of Italy. They reminded me of going on holiday when I was a kid, crammed into the back of the car, pinching my sisters and whining 'She started it' when my mum turned to give us a whack.

We travelled the east coast of Australia in our car and if we were well behaved my dad would stop at the Big Banana at Coffs Harbour and we'd be allowed to buy a souvenir. It always had to be something useful – a ruler or a pencil – and couldn't be anything frivolous like a sticker. It struck me that these families were doing the same thing, but these kids got to see the 'big' David or the 'big' Leaning Tower. From the glimpses I caught of their faces, though, crammed in the back and twisted with boredom, I could see they'd rather be back in the pool at the villa. Just like we used to wish we were back swimming at the beach.

Tuscany's most expensive spas and most exclusive resorts are in Saturnia, but my guidebook said there was a free place to bathe in hot sulphurated waters nearby at a place called Cascate del Gorello. It said it was a pretty spot with pools and rocks 'stained coppery green', and insinuated that it was a free and easy place where hippies wandered around naked in pigtails.

I arrived in Cascate del Gorello to find that it had been 'developed' somewhat since my guidebook had been published. There was a carpark out front and they had graded a road down to the springs. An enterprising local had built a changing room and was charging €2 to use it and a nearby shop sold warm soft drinks at grossly inflated prices. I had imagined a secluded cascade of hot water, with perhaps the odd naked hippie meditating. Instead it was a place with the ambience of a Sydney swimming pool on a hot Saturday afternoon. I wove down the road past people in towels, before turning around and heading off.

After Terme di Saturnia the landscape changed, becoming flat and dry, the soil a bleak white clay. I was in *tufa* territory, now, a place where fields and towns were carved out of the soft limestone rock. There were still vineyards, of course – we were still in Tuscany, after all – and it struck me as I was riding along that in all my time in Italy I hadn't visited a winery. A few kilometres later I saw a hand-painted sign saying 'Wine tasting today' so I turned in.

The winery was called Villa Corano and by the look of things had only been open for business for a year or two. The carpark was empty and the main building deserted. On hearing Sophia's engine a silver-haired chap came struggling out of the attached house, pulling his clothes on. He was in such a hurry that I figured I must have been the first person to turn in that day, maybe that week, and he was determined not to let me go.

The sign out the front was written in English, and I hoped that meant my language would be spoken and understood. It was hoping for too much, of course; this guy's English was worse than my Italian. The winery tour consisted of him pointing out the sparkly new metal vats and me telling him that they were *molto* shiny. He poured me a couple of glasses of wine and after making a show of rolling them around my mouth, I started simply tossing them back, as much to fill the awkward silences than anything else. When the silence became really painful I told him I'd buy two bottles of wine – one of his whites and one of his reds. I set off again feeling a little fuzzy with a two-pack of Villa Corano wine swinging from Sophia's bag-holder hook.

I don't remember much of the road after that – three glasses of wine on an empty stomach will do that to you – but I do remember my arrival in Pitigliano. Not only was my first sight of the place mindblowing – it's not everyday that you see a medieval city sprouting out of a high volcanic outcrop like a stand of mushrooms – but I also was stung by a bee for the first time on my trip.

I'd been peppered by bugs every day since I'd left Milan. Sometimes it was hard-bodied ones, and their impact would sting if Sophia was travelling at speed (or at her version of it). But mostly they just squished against my shirt. As I was approaching Pitigliano, however, a bee flew in through the collar of my open-neck shirt and stung me on the chest. When I stopped to take photos of Pitigliano at a lookout point just the other side of the Lente River ten minutes later, I could hardly see through my camera's viewfinder. My eyes were still watering.

Gorges carved by the river surround Pitigliano on three sides and the town can only be approached by a road that winds its way up beside the man-made fort on the east side. The cliff here is riddled with caves cut out of the soft *tufa*, that were turned into medieval lock-ups that local Arthur Daleys would fill with wine, oil and whatever else they could turn a few bob on.

I found a room for the night in a house on the other side of the town, run by a woman who told me that the *butteri* used to earn a bit of extra cash in the 1970s by playing bit parts in spaghetti westerns.

I sat on a wall out front and watched the sun set over Pitigliano. As the light dulled, the demarcation between building and rock blurred and the town became a kind of primeval blob. I can't say that I warmed to the place. In 1622 the Jews in the town were forced to move into a tiny ghetto and were persecuted until they were finally forced to leave by the Fascists in 1938. It seemed to me that the town's dark past cast an uneasy pall over it.

Just before I went to sleep that night Sally texted me to say she'd bought herself a Kinder Surprise at lunch. 'It was a Smurf,' she texted. 'You'd have hated it.' Then, almost as an afterthought, she added that a Smurf was three apples tall.

I should point out that Sally is not usually one for peppering her text messages with interesting facts about little blue folk in white pants. It was just that at one stage in our journey through Italy together we'd had a heated discussion about how high a Smurf is. It wasn't an argument, but things did get tense for a while. I'd said they were life-size, meaning that they were as tall as you'd expect them to be, about the size of a dwarf. Sally disagreed, claiming that they were only an inch or two tall at most. Neither of us had proof to support our hypotheses, so we agreed to disagree. But obviously it was an issue that burned deeply within Sally, and she had visited the official Smurf website – www.smurf.com – and found the answer.

'Three apples tall, huh?' I said to myself before I went to sleep that night. 'Who'd have thought it?'

I didn't like to admit it to myself but I was missing Sally terribly. I found myself pointing out a medieval town on a distant hilltop or a field of sunflowers and then realising she wasn't there to see it. Or wishing that she was there to wrap her arms around my waist and rest her head on my back as I rode along. But it was silly things I missed most. Like the way she got really angry every time she got another kitchen pot soldier in her Kinder Surprise. Or the ridiculous song about Padre Pio that she sang to the tune of 'Hallelujah'.

I woke up just after midnight in a panic that Sally wasn't lying next to me. At first I thought she was in the bathroom, but then I realised with a sigh that she was back in England. The only way I could get back to sleep was by humming 'Padre Pio' to myself.

The next day I left Tuscany and entered Lazio. It was the end of July and farmers were pulling everything out of the ground in anticipation of *ferragosto*, the one month at the height of summer when most of Italy closes down for a break. They were burning their crops or ploughing them back into the soil, and I realised for the first time that my trip had nearly come to an end. Spring and the early days of summer were over. The time of harvest and abundance had passed. And Rome, the end of my trip, was only two days away.

To be honest, I was at the point in my journey where I just wanted to get to Rome. I didn't necessarily want the trip to be over. I just wanted to reach the Eternal City and still be in the mood to enjoy it. I figured I could get as far as Viterbo that night and then travel the 80 odd kilometres to Rome the next day.

But the farmers of Lazio seemed to have other ideas. I spent most of the morning stuck behind tractors carting trailers full of potatoes. They appeared one after another out of nowhere in Grotte di Castro, laden high with spuds covered in rich brown dirt. They formed a convoy, as they headed to the spud factory, and they crawled along at a speed that seemed painfully slow, even by Sophia's lazy standards.

Other cars came up behind me and overtook me and the tractors, passing the whole convoy in one fell swoop. Sophia, however, had neither the energy nor the inclination. On the few occasions I was able to coax sufficient velocity from her another vehicle would approach from the opposite direction or we'd come upon a blind curve.

So I spent most of the morning sitting behind them, breathing in the rich aroma of freshly turned dirt and dodging the odd potato dislodged by a jolt from a pothole.

As I wound down the hill from San Lorenzo Nuovo towards the shore of Lago di Bolsena I spotted a sign for the Via Francigena, pointing up a dirt road. It was the same sign I had seen on my first days in the mountains south of Milan and seeing the little cartoon monk in a robe that was the icon for the Via Francigena produced a wave of nostalgia that made me turn onto the road without thinking.

It turned out to be quite a pilgrimage. The road climbed up a hill beside a chain-wire fence and through an olive field, where a pack of dogs chased after me, nipping at my heels. It petered out to a sandy path that became a rocky one and then disappeared altogether. Just when I thought I was lost another sign featuring the little monk miraculously appeared and I set off again. I ended up in a bramble patch, where a startled group of hikers were surprised and amused to see an old Vespa on their walking track, and finally in a vast field of dead or dying sunflowers. I got a dull feeling in the pit of my stomach that my journey was nearly over. I made my way back to the main road and continued south.

It was dark when I reached Viterbo but from what I saw as I entered the grimy city gates, I wasn't missing much. The city had once been the seat of the papacy, but it had the bejesus bombed out of it during World War II. I stayed in a hotel that looked like it was the set of an old-fashioned American crime movie and spent the night watching dreadful Italian television.

Actually, that's not strictly true. I watched *The Nanny* dubbed into Italian. Watching television shows dubbed into another language makes you realise just how much of the show's impact comes from the actors' voices. I remember watching *Skippy the Bush Kangaroo* in Iran. It had been dubbed into Farsi and they'd given Sonny's father, Ranger Matt Hammond, the gruff, stern voice of a ruthless Ayatollah. It was a million miles removed from the character's usual genial tones and it changed my perception of him altogether.

I had the same problem with the Italian version of *The Nanny*. They got the tone of the voices of Mr Sheffield and Niles right, but the others, especially Fran the nanny, were way off. They'd given Fran a deep, sultry voice, fundamentally altering the dynamics of the show. Fran's whiny voice is the whole point of the show, anyway, but the Italian dubbers obviously couldn't bring themselves to give such an attractive woman such an unattractive voice.

The Nanny was followed by an Italian show where couples read poetry and sang to each other to express their feelings. I found I could only watch it for a few moments at a time before feeling nauseous and flicked over to Italian MTV until my stomach settled. That was a disappointment, too. The two female reporters who roamed Italian beaches in their bikinis and seemed to be on every other time I'd watched were gone and Red Hot Chilli Peppers and Avril Lavigne were on high rotation.

I set off for Rome early the next morning, breaking my journey for a coffee in Sutri, a town famous for its Etruscan tombs. It is less than 50 kilometres from Rome and was one of the last stops on the medieval pilgrim trail to the capital. I parked Sophia out the front of the local real-estate agent and found a café that looked like an Italian version of the bar in *Cheers*. The breezy waitress greeted everybody by name and presented them with their order before they had even asked for it. I ordered a *macchiato* and a Kinder Surprise and I'm sure if I had returned the next day both would be waiting for me on the counter when I came in.

On my return I found two women admiring Sophia. One woman was considerably older than the other and wore a scarf on her head. When she realised the bike was mine she spoke to me in Italian, hurriedly and excitedly. I explained that I was Australian and couldn't speak much Italian. Her daughter translated what she was saying.

'She says it is the Vespa of her youth!' she explained.

I told the daughter my story – how I found Sophia on the Internet, how I was riding her from Milan to Rome – and she translated it for her mother. Her mother reached up and squeezed my cheek with a smile, tears welling in her eyes. Seeing Sophia had transported her back to a time when she was young and free and when the boys wanted her. I can't imagine a Holden Commodore having the same effect in forty years' time.

The final 30 kilometres along the S2 to Rome reminded me an awful lot of the expressway south of Sydney. The road cut through rolling dry hills that were surprisingly empty of houses and other buildings. The land here had been owned until 1980 by the Collegio Germanico, set up in the second half of the sixteenth century to promote Catholicism in Germany, and had never been divided up. The lack of houses and buildings is unusual in central Italy.

When I hit the outer suburbs it was like Sydney, too. There were garden centres and strip malls with Chinese restaurants and hairdressers. Except here in Rome you'd spot the odd tomb or temple, thousands of years old, in the middle of it all. The driving was a little crazier, too. One guy tailgated me for a kilometre, overtook on a blind bend and then turned into a garden centre almost immediately. I could tell my *vaffanculo* arm would be getting a bit of a work-out in Rome.

Finally the S2 hit the River Tiber and I came upon the Rome I'd been expecting. The bridge that spanned the river here was blindingly white and lined with huge white marble statues that looked imperial and triumphant. Anywhere else such a bridge would have looked ridiculous. But here, in Rome, beside stadia built in a similar style for the 1960 Olympics, it looked right.

The 1960 Rome Olympics were a special showcase for Italian-made products. More than 100 Vespas were made available to athletes in the Olympic village. Apparently organisers had a hard time getting the Italian middle-weight boxer Nino Benvenuti to share his. And Canadian sprinter Harry Jerome, the 100-metre record holder, was often seen buzzing recklessly around the village at all hours. Mister Selfridge, the president of Sears, Roebuck & Co, the US retailer, was in Rome to watch the Olympics and was so impressed by the Vespas that he began making inquiries about importing them to America.

I rode along the east side of the Tiber towards the heart of the city. It's always difficult to get your bearings in a big city. In smaller towns you can follow pretty much any road and know that sooner or later you'll hit the town centre. In a city, though, that's not a given, so I always look for a landmark, find it on my map and then take it from there.

In Rome the problem was that there are just too many landmarks. Even places that aren't really important enough to put on a Lonely Planet map, like the Naval Academy, for example, are so impressive-looking that I spent a good ten minutes trying to find it on my map, convinced that a building so grand had to be marked. In the end I decided to follow the signs to the Vatican City and take it from there. I'd visited Rome fifteen years before and, if I remembered rightly, St Peter's was just on the other side of the river from the centre of the city.

As I approached St Peter's I spotted a bridge to the other part of the city, Castel Sant'Angelo, on my left. Soon I was in the heart of old Rome, rattling up Corso Vittorio Emmanuele II, looking out for street signs but being constantly distracted by some of the greatest buildings the world has ever seen. The Typewriter Building (the Vittorio Emmanuel Monument). Trajan's Markets. The Forum. In the end I gave up and just rode, rattled by cobblestones and laughing at just how amazing it all was. I was riding through Rome, the Eternal City, on a forty-year-old Vespa. How cool was that?

I rode up Via dei Fori Imperiali to the Colosseum and parked Sophia on the forecourt there, beside a gelato van. I had booked a room in a hotel on Via Palestro, up near the Stazione Centrale Roma Termini, Rome's central railway station, figuring it would be easy to find. I looked at my map and it was. I headed back up Fori Imperiali, turned right onto Via Cavour and a minute or so later I was as good as there.

The hotel was surprisingly nice, set above a restaurant with small tables that spilled out onto the pavement, forcing pedestrians to step out onto the street and into the path of passing motor scooters. When I entered the hotel the restaurant was empty and the waiters sat bored at the tables. But when the sun went down the diners started appearing. I could hear the change from my room. The scrape of chairs, the clink of glasses and the hub-bub of conversation grew louder and louder.

Around nine, a man with an accordion came to serenade the diners. His selection of tunes was particularly gratifying. He played all the classics – 'Volare', 'That's Amore', 'O Sole Mio' – and I drifted off to sleep a happy man. It was corny. It was clichéd. But it seemed so right.

CHAPTER SEVENTEEN

Rome

Kinder Surprise Toy: Green Vespa
(K02-028)

The publicity department at Piaggio likes to claim that there wasn't an actor or an actress in the 1950s and 1960s who didn't ride a Vespa 'at least once'. What's more, they have the evidence to prove it. Deep inside the archives that line the walls of the Vespa Museum in Pontedera they have photos of all kinds of movie stars astride a Vespa. Rock Hudson. William Holden. Henry Fonda. Paul Newman. Charlton Heston. Even big blokes like Anthony Quinn, Gary Cooper and John Wayne, who you'd think wouldn't want to be seen dead on a motor scooter. The ladies are well represented, too, with snapshots of a Vespa-riding Brigitte Bardot, Marilyn

Monroe, Angie Dickenson, Jayne Mansfield and, of course, Sophia Loren, just to name a few.

It helped that all the biggest movies of the time, such as *Ben Hur*, *Spartacus* and *Quo Vadis*, were filmed at the Cinecittà studios on the outskirts of Rome. Hollywood stars were 'forced' to spend months at a time in Rome and quickly learnt that the best way to get around the city was on a Vespa, supplied, most likely, by the canny folk in the Piaggio publicity department. I picked up a great poster on my first day in Rome of Charlton Heston astride a Vespa in his full *Ben Hur* outfit. It was the same model Vespa as Sophia.

Of course, Vespas starred in movies, too. The curvaceous little beauty from Pontedera made her film debut in 1950 in *Domenica d'Agosto*, one of Marcello Mastroianni's early movies. By 1962 Vespas had appeared in sixty-four movies, and even today you'll see them popping up on the big screen. Not just in period pieces, such as *The Talented Mr Ripley*, but in the recent Eddie Murphy flop *I Spy*, and the teen romance *The Lizzie McGuire Movie*. The new model ET4 made its film debut in *102 Dalmations*.

Of course, the most famous celluloid Vespa is the one Gregory Peck and Audrey Hepburn rode in *Roman Holiday*. Audrey Hepburn won an Oscar for her role as the repressed princess who falls in love in Rome, but *Forbes* magazine claims the Oscar should have been given to the Vespa. 'While Gregory Peck was courting

Hepburn,' it noted, 'the rest of the world was falling in love with the other "she", the Vespa.'

The movie was directed by Hollywood legend William Wyler, and the scenes featuring a carefree Peck and Hepburn buzzing around Rome on a metallic green Vespa 125 became an international symbol of romance and freedom. Costantino Sambuy, the CEO of Piaggio USA, insisted that a poster of the movie hang in every showroom in the States. And every souvenir stall in Rome sells badly reproduced pictures from that movie as well as *Roman Holiday* calendars with a different image from the movie for each month. They know that the movie summed up the essence of falling in love in this amazing city. The 'lightness of being', to quote Mr Sambuy, and that heady feeling of romantic escape.

I certainly felt a 'lightness of being' on my first full day in Rome but it wasn't because of any notion of romantic escape. Rather, it was brought on by the cobblestones. In Rome they are small and square, about the size of a matchbox, with a tendency to sink to a variety of levels. On a small bike like Sophia it created a bone-shaking effect, and my bum was numb in no time at all.

I'd got up early the next day, excited to be in Rome, and had ridden around the city as it woke up. *Apes* scuttled through the cobbled streets, delivering milk and fresh vegetables. Café owners swept the pavement or served men in suits on their way to the office. On a corner a priest chatted with a parishioner about the coming weekend football matches and a flock of nuns breezed across the road, bringing the early morning traffic to a stop.

It struck me that Rome has a different demeanour to all the other Italian cities I had passed through. It is confident. It has business to do and it just goes ahead and does it. The ruins from its past give the city a feeling of space that many other great cities lack, and like most visitors to Rome I got the distinct feeling that Romans consider them part of the furniture. Tourists, too, are regarded like the sparrows that flit about the piazzas and thoroughfares. Part of the scenery, largely ignored and shooed away when they get too close.

I had a cappuccino in a café on Via Margutta. One of my favourite parts of *Roman Holiday* was when Audrey Hepburn decided to have a go at riding the Vespa herself and crashed into the painters' easels set up there. She made running over a hawker and his cart look like fun. Indeed, even the hawkers and painters and local constabulary looked like they enjoyed it. As a seventeen-year-old living in the western suburbs of Sydney I remember ruing the fact that the New South Wales police force would not have been so understanding if I was similarly reckless in my Datsun 120Y.

Little has changed on Via Margutta since they filmed the movie. When I mounted the footpath and parked beside the café the policeman on the opposite corner didn't even bat an eyelid. If a time machine dumped

someone on Via Margutta at that moment they'd spot
Sophia parked beside a quaint café, and figure they
were back in the 1960s.

I stood at the marble bar, beside an espresso machine
that had more chrome than Sophia, and was overcome
with a nagging feeling that, as wonderful as Rome was,
something was missing. I couldn't quite put my finger
on it until a young couple rode past on a new ET4. I
needed one more vital ingredient to make my Roman
Holiday perfect. I had the City. I had the Vespa. All I
needed was my very own Audrey Hepburn. (*You* know.
Sally!) I drained the last of my coffee, grabbed another
bombolone for the road and called into the laundromat
around the corner. It doubled as an Internet café and I
used one of their computers to book Sally a return
ticket to Rome that weekend.

Sally's flight was due to arrive at Rome's Fiumicino airport at 7 pm on Friday evening so I set off just after five
to give myself a bit of time, just in case something went
wrong. It was lucky I did. Just past EUR, the suburb
Mussolini built to showcase Fascist architecture, the
traffic was suddenly bumper to bumper, as everyone
escaped to the coast for the weekend.

The road to the airport and the coast is gun-barrel straight and on 9 February 1951 Piaggio set the world speed record for a motor scooter there. A specially tuned Vespa called the Siluro (torpedo) was clocked by representatives from the International Motorcycle Federation doing 174.418 kilometres an hour. I followed the lead of the other scooters weaving through the traffic but we all got stuck behind an oversized truck that blocked the lane and the verge on the side as well. I wouldn't be setting any land speed benchmarks that evening. The Siluro's record was safe.

As the sun set over the ruins of Ostia Antica, I flicked on Sophia's headlight and noticed with alarm that it wasn't working. It wasn't totally dark yet and I was only 3 kilometres from Fiumicino, so getting to the airport wouldn't be a problem. Nor would getting back to Rome, even if I couldn't fix the light. There was a train that went from the airport directly to Stazione Termini, very close to our hotel.

I hoped that the cobblestones had simply shaken a wire loose and fixing the problem would be as easy as reattaching it. Abandoning Sophia at the airport and using the train instead wasn't what I'd had in mind. It wasn't very *Roman Holiday*. I couldn't imagine Gregory Peck turning up and saying to Audrey Hepburn that instead of a carefree day on a Vespa he thought they'd catch a crowded train instead.

I parked Sophia just outside the Arrivals Hall and

checked the board. Sally's plane was going to be an hour late so I used the time to disassemble the headlight and check the wires. They seemed to be connected okay so I replaced the bulb with a spare one that Marco had given me to keep for emergencies. 'They always go at night,' he had said wisely. 'So it is best to keep a spare!' The headlight worked and I said a prayer of thanks to Marco, my Mary fridge magnet and Padre Pio, the saint Marco had recommended to me as being fresh and raring to go. By the time I had cleaned myself up, leaving a rather unsightly grease mark on the roller-towel in the toilets, Sally's plane had arrived.

She emerged lugging a bag that was twice the size of the bag she'd brought to Tuscany for two weeks. 'I figured we wouldn't be carrying your bag,' she said. 'And besides, we're in Rome. I need shoes!'

The ride back to the city centre in the crisp evening air was invigorating and within moments it felt like Sally had never left. She rested her hands on my knees and her chin on my shoulder, leaving them there until we reached Porta San Paolo and the start of the cobblestones. I took her on a whistlestop tour of Rome by night, past the Vittorio Emmanuel Monument, along the Via dei Fori Imperiali beside the ancient Roman Forum, before finally pulling up in front of the Colosseum.

Sally was suitably impressed. 'Wow!' she said with a wide-eyed grin. 'It's so *Roman*!'

When we got back to our room the accordion player was right under the window. He was playing all the classics again and Sally accused me of having paid him. I cracked open the bottle of red I'd bought at Villa Corano near Pitigliano and had been lugging around ever since. Sally described it as 'a bit spicy'.

Later we drifted off to sleep as the man under our window played 'O Sole Mio'. I was hearing the lyrics for 'It's Now or Never' in my mind and smiled at how well my impulsive plan to bring Sally to Rome, now or never, had gone.

We began our weekend in Rome by having breakfast in Babington's Tea Rooms, an august establishment at the bottom of the Spanish Steps. It was opened in 1896 by the Babington sisters, Anna Maria and Isabel Cargill, and is the sort of place you'd expect to see Maggie Smith fussing about in. The Black Cat logo hasn't changed since the 1960s and neither, it seemed, had Babington's. It had a faded, curling-at-the-edges Englishness and seemed a bit like a sandwich that had been left out on the counter too long.

'It reminds me of a seedy hotel in Bridlington,' whispered Sally. 'I bet they have salad cream.'

The waitresses, old spinsters from the 1960s, too, by the look of them, wore faded green uniforms, and served our scones and cream in a fussy, complicated manner.

As we ate, a fruitfly buzzed around our heads and Sally confessed that she knew how to sex it. She had learnt the skill in biology lessons at school. 'Boy ones have pointy bottoms,' she opined. 'Girl ones have round bottoms.'

The rest of our day in Rome, I am pleased to report, was much, much better. It passed like a movie directed by William Wyler, a slide show of Roman sights from the back of a buzzing old Vespa. Sophia really was the perfect guide to the Eternal City. We zipped up tiny lanes with washing strung between them, past the craftsmen on Via dell'Orso repairing chandeliers and making gilt frames and right up to the door of ancient monuments. When we ate lunch in a café overlooking the Pantheon, I was able to park Sophia with a group of other scooters only metres away.

After lunch we made a pilgrimage to Via Veneto, a lazy curve of road that descends from Porta Pinciana to Piazza Barberini. It was the most glamorous road in Rome in the 1960s and its cafés and bars were the haunts of movie stars. They in turn were haunted by the paparazzi, who swarmed here on Vespas, looking for the scandalous photograph that would make them their fortune. The film stars have gone now. They have all decamped to the more bohemian vibe of Trastevere.

While we were on Via Veneto I wanted to take Sally to my favourite place in Rome, Santa Maria della Concezione. It is just up from Piazza Barberini, and from the outside it looks like nothing more than another unassuming seventeenth-century church. But underneath, in the crypt, are a series of underground chapels decorated in a style you'll never see on *Changing Rooms*. Between 1528 and 1870 the monks of a very peculiar Capuchin order decided to brighten the place up with the bones of their dead brethren.

Gregory Peck never took Audrey Hepburn to Santa Maria della Concezione in *Roman Holiday*. I'm not sure what a young princess would make of a chandelier made from ribs and vertebrae. Nor do I think she would have appreciated the messages some of the monks left behind. 'What you are, we used to be,' read one. 'What we are, you will be.' Not the sort of thing a young princess with a life of selfless royal duty ahead of her would like to hear. A visit here would have seen the princess in therapy, I think.

Sally, however, loved it. She was a nurse before going into publicity and marvelled at how tackily macabre it all was. She wandered through the crypts, identifying the different bones and impressed by the way the monks had used them. 'I would never have used a pelvic girdle to make a ceiling rosette,' she said. 'But somehow it works.'

You weren't allowed to take photographs in the crypt – the monks had a nice little postcard concession going, you see – and the brother at the entrance desk had the difficult task of enforcing the rule. He'd call out when he spotted an offender, but more often than not they'd ignore him. Periodically he'd leave his desk to counsel them personally. I wondered if he used the quiet times to sketch out a few preliminary ideas about how he'd like his own bones arranged. If his fellow monks had a sense of humour – and the crypt suggested that they did, albeit a very black one – they'd arrange him into a 'No Photos!' sign.

Another high point of the day was when we swept around the Vittorio Emmanuel Monument and onto Fori Imperiali, with the Colosseum up ahead. In daylight I felt more confident and tackled the bend at speed, weaving in and out of the traffic like I was Charlton Heston on a chariot in *Ben Hur*. Sally dug her fingers into my thighs so hard she nearly drew blood.

She never really got used to the traffic in Rome. After the gentle drives on the back roads of Tuscany and living in London, she found it scary and chaotic. There didn't seem to be any kind of order, she said. It was crazy and people didn't seem to follow any sort of definable road rules.

I'd thought that on my first day in Rome, too. The traffic on Via Cavour had looked like a scramble of ants after their nest has been disturbed. But after an hour of being honked at and told what to do with various intimate parts of my anatomy I discovered there were rules or, rather, one simple rule. If you had a scooter you could ride wherever you damn well pleased. You just made sure you did it with a confidence that told every other driver on the road that's what you were doing.

The realisation was quite liberating, actually. I started riding on the inside of cars, the outside of cars and anywhere between them. If there was a queue of traffic, I'd ride a couple of hundred metres down the wrong side of the road to get around it. The abuse stopped and the people driving cars became more courteous, giving me a few millimetres more to squeeze by. I got where I wanted to go quicker and arrived in a less rattled state. Basically, I had to forget everything that I'd been taught at the Motorcycle Riding Centre in Sydney.

It's an attitude tourists visiting Rome should adopt when they cross a road. Just step out and sail across. It's what the nuns do. And who's ever heard that riddle 'What's black and white and red all over?' answered 'A nun dead in the middle of Piazza Navona after being hit by a Fiat'?

Okay, I did get a little carried away at times. I nearly hit a policewoman on Via Nazionale near the roundabout at Piazza della Repubblica. It's a restricted traffic zone there, and overhead cameras regulate who can use it, so the policewoman stepped out, blowing her whistle, to try to stop me entering. When I spotted that she was just Vigili Urbani, Municipal Police, I wove around her and kept going. If she could make out the numbers on Sophia's old battered numberplate, if she could be even bothered writing a ticket and sending it, well, I'd deal with it then.

'You better not do that when you get back to London,' said Sally, a little shocked by my behaviour. 'I don't think the authorities will be so forgiving if you try to evade the congestion charge.' Secretly, though, I think she was impressed by my new Mediterranean approach to road rules.

That night we ate in Trastevere, one of Rome's most lively quarters. According to my guidebook it was the place where movie stars hung out these days, now that the bars and cafés of Via Veneto had become passé. I told Sally that with a little luck we might spot Brad Pitt unwinding over an espresso after a hard day's shopping for a new ring for Jen. Or we might catch a glimpse of George Clooney sharing a Campari or two with mates after launching a new fleet of motor scooter ambulances. At worst, we'd get a cheap feed in a part of town dripping with good old Roman *brio*.

Trastevere has always been a fiercely independent section of Rome. The name comes from *trans Tiberim*, across the Tiber, and the locals still refer to themselves as *noantri* – we others. Old-timers rarely cross the river. As soon as we did, weaving through groups of people out for a good time, you could feel the buzz.

I parked Sophia with a group of other scooters outside Santa Maria in Trastevere, probably the first official

Christian place of worship built in Rome. The piazza here was surrounded by lively bars and restaurants, but we wanted something a bit more intimate and plunged down one of the tiny alleyways that ran off it. Here the tables of rustic *trattorie* spilled out onto the pavements and we picked a restaurant that looked suitably charming. As we ate, the crowds in their stripey shirts and little black dresses continued to jostle past, close enough to pick at our food if they wanted to. The only downside was a guy selling lime-green glow sticks on the street in front of us. They weren't quite in keeping with the rustic ambience and threw a sickly hue over our food.

People claim that the Rome of *La Dolce Vita* and all those other great old black and white movies has disappeared. And strictly speaking, it has. The lively cafés and bars on Via Veneto that Marcello Mastroianni cruised with his paparazzi mates is now the domain of American businessmen on expense accounts. And Rugantino's, the nightclub near the Spanish Steps where his dad took a fancy to a leggy French dancer, has now famously become a McDonald's. But that night in Trastevere, with its lively crowds, cafés, and restaurants and kiosks selling slices of watermelon and *grattachecca*, flavoured ice, I felt that we had found it again. That *brio*, that liveliness that jumped off the screen and shook me as a fifteen-year-old boy.

In keeping with the movie theme of our day, Sally wanted to visit the Trevi Fountain. She loved the movie

Three Coins in a Fountain and wanted to see the world-famous fountain that it featured. 'You've never lived until you've loved in Rome!' she said, quoting the movie's tag line with a grin.

In the movie three American girls throw coins in the fountain and make a wish that they will meet the men of their dreams. The tradition is that if you throw a coin into the fountain, over your shoulder and facing away, you'll return to Rome. Toss a second coin and you'll fall in love with an Italian. A third will ensure that you marry them. I told Sally we could go as long as she promised to toss only one coin. The way I rode in Roman traffic was the only thing about me even remotely Italian.

A lot of people, it seems, want to return to Rome. And an awful lot of them want to marry an Italian. Only the day before police had arrested a homeless man called Roberto Cercelletta who was pulling out over €1000 from the fountain each day. The money was supposed to go to charity, but this guy was wading into the water at Neptune's feet and helping himself to it. The police claim that he'd been doing it since 1968 and I wondered why he was still homeless. He must have amassed a small fortune over the years.

We arrived and found quite a crowd contributing to Mr Cercelletta's retirement fund. Even though it was past midnight there were people ten deep at the rail ready to turn their back and toss their coins. Elsewhere people sat on the steps eating gelato. The souvenir sellers were doing a roaring trade, strangely in miniature alabaster statues of David.

Sally found the fountain bigger than she expected and the atmosphere a little more exuberant. 'It's like Leicester Square!' she said.

Almost on cue a pack of scousers on a buck's night jumped into the fountain and made like Anita Ekberg in *La Dolce Vita*. One of the guys, a large chap, even had breasts to rival Anita's.

As we left Sally tossed a coin and made a wish. I asked her what she wished for but she wouldn't say. 'If it comes true, you'll know,' she said with an enigmatic smile.

Sally's plane back to London left Fiumicino at five on Sunday afternoon. Once we factored in the one-hour ride out to the airport and the airline's requirement to check in two hours before departure we didn't have much time to see more of Rome. After rising late we simply popped out to St Peter's, where Sally spent a good deal of the morning debating whether to buy a Padre Pio statue or not. She ended up deciding against it. It was surprisingly heavy for its size and the padre's eyebrows were painted in such a fashion that he looked cross.

The traffic was lighter on the road to the airport but

there were roadworks and we were diverted along the coast through Lido di Castel Fusano and Lido di Ostia. It added twenty minutes to the journey but we still arrived there with time in hand.

Our weekend in Rome had been as brief as the one shared by Gregory Peck and Audrey Hepburn, and just as romantic. We had buzzed along cobbled streets, eaten beside ancient monuments and thrown coins in the Trevi Fountain. But like Audrey's character in *Roman Holiday*, Sally had to go back to work. Not as a princess, but as a publicist on a new book. The carefree holiday was over.

It was easier saying goodbye this time than it had been in Pisa a few weeks before. Then I was only half-way through my journey from Milan to Rome on a 1961 Vespa. Now that journey was nearly over.

I stayed in Rome for just another two days. Now that the August holidays had started most businesses were closed and the city had turned into a ghost town. The restaurant below was shuttered and locked, the tables and chairs packed away. The Internet laundromat was closed and so too were many of the little cafés and *alimentari*. Only businesses catering exclusively to foreign tourists seemed to open.

The fact that Italy closed down in August helped put a fullstop at the end of my trip. The temptation would have been to keep going, to follow new roads, but I know that I would have ended up missing Sally and not enjoying it so much. This way I could finish my trip on a high, content that it had met all my expectations and in many ways exceeded them.

The Eurailers were still flooding into Rome so at least the shops at Stazione Termini were still open. I had a coffee and a *bombolone* in a small café there and called into the sweet shop for a final Kinder Surprise. They had one tray of summer Kinder Surprises left. I picked out different ones, holding them to my ear and shaking them to try to get a clue as to what was inside. The woman at the counter gave me a strange look so I quickly picked out two and bought them.

I opened them back at the hotel. One was a Smurf – Papa Smurf, with a megaphone to be exact. The other, to my great delight, was another green Vespa. I put it together and placed it on the bed as I gathered my things and wondered if that was what Sally had wished for when she tossed her coin into the Trevi Fountain.

I thought back over the past two-and-a-half months and realised that I'd already got what I wished for a long time ago. A summer in Italy on a Vespa with too much chrome and a pretty girl riding on the back.

Life doesn't get much better than that.

EPILOGUE

I left for Milan a few days after Sally flew back to London. By keeping to the biggest major roads I was allowed to travel on, it took me two days to cover the same distance I had taken three months to travel in the opposite direction. It seemed that, if she was pushed, Sophia could be counted on to perform. Either that or she knew she was heading home to a garage where she could rest again.

Over those forty-eight hours Italy continued to confound and amaze me. One hundred kilometres from Siena, in an area of bleak barren fields, I filled up at a Tamoil petrol station that kept a prairie dog on a leash. At another petrol station, in the middle of the day, I had to use a Bankomat bowser that gave me a receipt for the amount I hadn't used. When I tried to redeem it at another Agip service station I was told I could only redeem it at the petrol station I had used, hundreds of kilometres away.

I stopped at Livorno to see Marco, walking into his workshop unannounced like I had when Sally first went back to London. He was still working on the Spanish Primavera and was genuinely touched when I presented him with the Kinder Surprise Vespa I found in Rome. He admitted he'd been trying to get one, too, without much luck. He put it in his display cabinet, giving it pride of place.

I spent that night in the hostel at Lucca and tackled the Apennines the next day, taking the S62. It was a beautiful drive through the mountains and I followed it all the way to Parma. It wasn't as adventurous as the route I had taken before but I reached the Po Plains without incident. By late afternoon I was in Milan and back at the Hotel Virgilio, near the station. The little old manager was on holidays, so it wasn't quite the same.

Gianni was arranging to ship Sophia to Australia for me, but before he did I wanted to go back to Lake Como and finish the journey around the lake that I had started but never finished. I rode up the east side of the lake this time, to Bellagio, following an old Moto Guzzi scooter that backfired a lot. The guy eventually pulled over and waved me past. I knew what he was going through.

I ate lunch in a small restaurant high above the lake called the Three Roses, and caught the motor ferry across the lake to Menaggio. When I pulled up at the hostel both Dave and Alberto walked out, smiling and shaking their heads. Dave was the barman now and had introduced €1 shots. I spent the night there but don't remember much about it.

I rode back down to Milan the next day. Gianni was waiting for me at his office, ready to take Sophia back before joining his family on the lake for the summer holidays. The traffic in Milan didn't seem as daunting and I fancifully thought it was because I had become almost Italian. Gianni quickly nipped that idea in the bud by telling me that in August Milan is a ghost town. Everyone is on holiday.

I took Gianni to lunch in the restaurant nearby that he had taken me to on the day we sorted out Sophia's paperwork. He shook his head at my tales. He never thought Sophia would make it to Rome. I told him that if it hadn't been for his generosity, and the generosity of people like Marco and Filippo, she never would have.

I guess I've also got to thank Sophia for that. She inspired people and charmed them and reminded them just what it was that they loved about Vespas. She gave Sally and me an unforgettable two weeks together, cementing our relationship. And, more importantly, Sophia showed me a side of Italy –

and the Italians – that I would have otherwise missed.

You've got to love a motor scooter for that.

THE END

THE VROOM WITH A VIEW SLIDE SHOW

Courtesy of the World Wide Web, you too can make the journey from Milan to Rome on the back of an old Vespa, without getting a speck of oil on your hands, simply by visiting www.petermoore.net.

Just follow the links to the Vroom with a View slide show and before you know it you'll be ring-a-ding-a-linging past fields of sunflowers and hilltop medieval towns and carousing at pine-nut festivals with long-legged Martini girls. Crack open a bottle of chianti, put on an old Dean Martin CD and you've got the whole Italy-on-a-Vespa experience.

While you're there, check out the websites for Peter's other books, or subscribe to his online newsletter for up-to-date information and your chance to win an autographed copy of one of his books.

See you at www.petermoore.net. Ciao!

A SELECTED LIST OF TRAVEL WRITING
AVAILABLE FROM BANTAM BOOKS

81341 2	LIFE IN A POSTCARD	Rosemary Bailey	£7.99
81523 7	THE MAN WHO MARRIED A MOUNTAIN	Rosemary Bailey	£7.99
81556 3	IT'S NOT ABOUT THE TAPAS	Polly Evans	£6.99
81557 1	KIWIS MIGHT FLY	Polly Evans	£6.99
81479 6	FRENCH SPIRITS	Jeffrey Greene	£6.99
81613 6	A YEAR OF RUSSIAN FEASTS	Catherine Cheremeteff Jones	£6.99
81490 7	BEST FOOT FORWARD	Susie Kelly	£6.99
81620 9	TWO STEPS BACKWARDS	Susie Kelly	£7.99
81601 2	HOLY COW!	Sarah Macdonald	£6.99
81250 5	BELLA TUSCANY	Frances Mayes	£6.99
81611 X	UNDER THE TUSCAN SUN	Frances Mayes	£7.99
81701 9	THE FULL MONTEZUMA	Peter Moore	£7.99
81700 0	THE WRONG WAY HOME	Peter Moore	£7.99
81736 1	NO SHITTING IN THE TOILET	Peter Moore	£7.99
81452 4	SWAHILI FOR THE BROKEN-HEARTED	Peter Moore	£6.99
81635 7	MONSOON DIARY	Shoba Narayan	£7.99
81448 6	TAKE ME WITH YOU	Brad Newsham	£6.99
81602 0	ALL THE RIGHT PLACES	Brad Newsham	£6.99
81551 2	THE BIG YEAR	Mark Obmascik	£6.99
81417 6	THE GREAT WHITE PALACE	Tony Porter	£7.99
81550 4	FOUR CORNERS	Kira Salak	£6.99
81566 0	FROM HERE, YOU CAN'T SEE PARIS	Michael Sanders	£7.99
81356 0	ON PERSEPHONE'S ISLAND	Mary Taylor Simeti	£7.99
81465 6	BITTER ALMONDS	Mary Taylor Simeti & Maria Grammatico	£6.99
81584 9	WITHOUT RESERVATIONS: THE TRAVELS OF AN INDEPENDENT WOMAN	Alice Steinbach	£7.99
81656 X	EDUCATING ALICE	Alice Steinbach	£7.99
81668 3	THE BONE MAN OF BENARES	Terry Tarnoff	£6.99
81532 6	CUBA DIARIES	Isadora Tattlin	£6.99
81555 5	AN EMBARRASSMENT OF MANGOES	Ann Vanderhoof	£7.99
81439 7	LEARNING TO FLOAT	Lili Wright	£6.99